Unlucky

Alf

Dene Lindley

The Derwent Press
Derbyshire, England

Unlucky Alf
By
Dene Lindley

ISBN 10: 1-84667-032-2
ISBN 13: 978-1-84667-032-9

Cover photo, back cover photo and author portrait by:
Steve Place, Creative Images Photography
Email: info@creativeimagesphotography.co.uk

Book design by: Pam Marin-Kingsley, www.far-angel.com

Published in 2008

by
The Derwent Press
Derbyshire, England

For Megan Davies

"Always Making Memories"

Acknowledgements

Living with writers can be very frustrating and at times incredibly boring. The reason I know this is mainly due to my wife and children constantly telling me. To this end I would sincerely like to thank my soul-mate Kate, and my children Samantha and Marcus for their never ending support and understanding.

Special thanks go out to Craig Lindley and Kay Brough who did a superb job in putting me back on track. Joanne Stenton Covi, Jo Lindley, Joan and Charlie Dagless, Emma Holland, Peter and Maxine Davies, Jean and Geoff Launders, David and Kla Smith, Claire and Shaun Strachan, for their encouragement and advice.

In addition I would like to thank my great friends Tony Foster, Leo Martinson and Steve Place for help beyond the call of duty. Ross and Andy from the gym. Nina Whitehouse, Jonathan Webster, Philip and Celia Thompson, Derek and Karen Mapp, Paul and Sally Andrews, Trish Kapur, John Clarke and Jane Moore for their loyal friendship. Matt Bulcroft for his computer wizardry. Kevin Jones, Neil Oliver, Karl Shore and Mark Laksevics for being good eggs. Andy Taylor for having to put up with me, and being bored senseless on numerous occasions.

An added extra thanks to Pam Marin-Kingsley, Shawna Bernard, Coralie Hughes Jensen and Joti Bryant, for their fantastic support, expertise, guidance and encouragement. Women are obviously the superior sex.

And finally I am indebted to the seven personalities that live with me in my head, all of which have contributed massively to this project, some more than others! I'm sorry if I've forgotten any one, but my excuse is that I've suffered from amnesia for as long as I can remember.

Contents

Introduction

**I realised from an early age that
I was always in the shit;
it's just the depth that varied!**

This story is part fiction, part biographical, giving an insight into my first fourteen years growing up in a tough mining town in South Yorkshire during the 60's. The story chronicles the adventures and escapades that my fellow gang members and I experienced along the way, ranging from scrumping apples at Granny Fart's, to ferreting with my pet Obadiah, an 'extreme weasel'.

Implicitly believing everything anyone told me created more problems than solutions.

Eccentric relations add spice to the proceedings, highlighting real-life concerns such as bullying, prejudice, schizophrenia and alcohol abuse, to name but a few!

Seen through the eyes of an innocent yet streetwise child, it compares today's issues and dilemmas with those of yester year. The journey is full of mishaps and mayhem, depicting a child's viewpoint of life.

This voyage of self-discovery is sometimes painful, yet always tinged with humour.

I now believe that the key to living successfully, is to be able to laugh at yourself when the odds are stacked against you.

Dene Lindley, 2008.

Chapter 1

The Skint Years in Maltby, South Yorkshire.

If I had waited just sixty seconds before making my grand entrance, my life might have been normal.

According to my Nan, I was thrust onto this earth on the back of one of my mother's anal eruptions. The date was the 28th of December 1960, and the time was exactly 11:59 p.m. The midwife in charge of proceedings apparently passed out, either on account of the putrid stench or the sight of me. My entry caused pandemonium on the ward in Listerdale Maternity Home, in the County of South Yorkshire, owing to the speed and method in which I emerged. It was likened to a thunderous cannon backfiring—ear-piercing and threatening. But I had landed and my life was about to commence.

My mother often told me that I wasn't born, I was created. She had desperately tried not to acknowledge my existence, out of embarrassment. She hadn't realised that she was with child until eight months into the pregnancy, thinking she was merely suffering from bloating. I was a complete shock to her system, totally unexpected. My family was extremely poor, and another mouth to feed only exacerbated the situation. So, beatified with my mother's scorn and belonging to a family who pretended to like me, I set forth on Life's journey, looking forward with relish to the trials and tribulations I was destined to experience.

Today, when I seek answers to my many questions, I turn to the 'World Wide Webster'—the Internet gospel according to Jonathan P. Webster, a great friend of mine and the fount of all knowledge. (The only downside to this intellectual giant is that he suffers from having ginger hair and because of it, he is the only guy I have ever met who desperately wanted to go prematurely bald.)

The World Wide Webster states that on December 28th, all "Catalogues" (colloquial South Yorkshire term for Catholics) celebrate the Feast of the Holy Innocents, which commemorates the Massacre of the Innocents, ordered by King Herod. Realising he had been outwitted by the Magi and new born Jesus had slipped through his hands, Herod immediately gave orders to kill all boys in the Bethlehem area aged two years and under. Thus this was deemed the unluckiest day of the year.

Also on this day, the people on Minorca in the Balearic Isles celebrate their equivalent of April Fool's Day.

I have come to realise that if I wasn't born with bad luck, I would have no luck at all!

My mother spent all of five minutes choosing my Christian names, Alfred and Wilfred, whilst drinking copious amounts of milk stout. With my surname being Hart, when the names are linked together and shortened somewhat, they sound rather comical. "Alf Hart" said quickly in a Yorkshire accent comes across as "I'll fart." Better still, when both Alfred and Wilfred are shortened, it comes over as "Alf will fart." Either way, the kids at school had a ball with me, and blessed with this unfortunate sounding moniker, my life was mapped out for me at a very early age.

I've spent many hours pondering why my mother should have christened me with these names, knowing the stick I would get from other children. Maybe she inspired Johnny Cash to write one of his classics, 'A Boy Named Sue'. I did contemplate ways of murdering her and disposing of her body without anyone ever knowing. The problem I had was that my Mum was a very large, domineering lady, and to quote my uncle, Bernard, "I would rather fuck her than fight her." This left me with no choice but just to get on with my life the best way I could, though it was crap.

Grandad once said to me, "Cheer up, son, things could be worse."

So I cheered up, and things did get worse. Later on in my life, I took comfort from two other unfortunate souls who had also been blessed with wildly amusing names. I met a gentleman called John Dyer who, when answering the phone, said "Dyer here." And in the 80's, in Leeds my neighbour happened to be called Gloria Stits...

My first years were spent on Churchill Avenue in a two-bedroom flat in a small mining village in South Yorkshire. The house—more like a bedsit—puts the B in basic. We shared the property with several million ubiquitous and uninvited guests who only appeared at night. The uninvited guests where in fact bed-bugs and fleas, which resided in the property prior to our arrival, and begrudged having to share the bed with my brother and me.

They also left Indian burns or raw broken skin on our legs and faces each night, which was their way of giving us a good night kiss.

We were a poor family who had been granted unhappiness in all its different guises by the Big Man Upstairs. It still pisses me off when I hear people say, "We were poor, but we were happy." Being poor is shit—make no mistake about it.

I remember the flat always being cold. We had to run around the bedroom each night like demented chickens in our duffle coats just to keep from freezing. We actually slept in our coats, so you can imagine how we must have reeked. And of course we kept a pig in the bedroom as an air freshener…

Another experience that sticks in my mind from my early years is that of always being hungry. My staple diet consisted of plain brown sauce sarnies (sandwiches) without butter. You could always tell the more well-off kids, as they would have butter or maggie-ann (margarine) on theirs. Another veritable feast we would enjoy on most, if not all evenings, was a packet variety of pea soup; my Mum got a job lot from Uncle Dab's war rations. By the taste of the bloody stuff, I think it was from the Boer War. The snot-coloured liquid was vile and had an aroma of old socks, but at least it was hot. However, the following day after consuming the broth, we could shit through the eye of a needle, which was horrendous on swimming days at school.

(I know that anal humour is not everyone's cup of tea, but for my brother and me, it was a mandatory part of our childhood.)

Growing up in Maltby, South Yorkshire, in the Little London housing estate was an education in itself. Maltby has its historical roots in Roman times. It is mentioned in the Domesday Book as 'by-malt,' which roughly means bypass the village, or wave goodbye to it. Either option instructed you to steer well clear.

Little London was a part of Maltby that most of its residents pretended didn't exist. The square two-storey, brown brick flats resembled featureless prisons, and the surrounding neighbourhood wasn't much better. Occupants felt cooped up, like being in a penitentiary, but without the screws for company. The police seldom patrolled this area—for fear of being mugged. Other than a small river running through Maltby, the only other things that flowed were beer and blood—mainly on a Saturday night.

We once got offered a house swap to the Bronx area of New York, but the other family pulled out at the last minute, fearing they were getting a rough deal...

My fearless mother worked part-time as a scarecrow to save time in looking after her appearance, which she modelled on Worzel Gummidge, who was known to have a nasty nature and numerous different personalities depending on which head he was wearing. She also led rook shooting parties. At home she was very strict—to the extent that my brother Craig and I were never permitted to cross the road alone. We spent the first seven years of our lives dreaming of sacred tarmac and distant kerbstones. As I've previously mentioned, it was like being incarcerated.

We had a friend at the time called Bewwy who modelled himself after Batman. Dram, as he was commonly known, rarely talked, and when he did, he didn't say much. But he did live across the road from us and was granted permission to cross it whenever he felt like it. (This may sound trivial, but I bet if Nelson Mandela had been able to venture just a few yards beyond the walls of his cell during his imprisonment, he would have jumped at the chance.) We would watch in awe as Dram valiantly ambled carefree across the red zone, sometimes closing his eyes as he did so, sort of showing off a little in front of my brother and me. Though one time, he got knocked down by the dustbin lorry to our great amusement.

We also had a friend called Albert who would sit on our front step, doing bird impressions at six o'clock each morning. It never bothered us too much, but our old neighbour, Mester Halfmoon (Mester being a sign of more respect than the standard Mister), promptly came out at five past six one morning and leathered Albert with his old pit belt. (You wouldn't be allowed to do that now, mind you—come to think about it, you weren't really allowed to do it back then...) It was effective though, and Albert did stop the whistling until his next teeth came through, many of them having been knocked out.

Mester Halfmoon was a crazy old coot, and once told us that he had seen a six-foot grass snake eating a kitten in our back garden. This absolutely terrified me, and I insisted on wearing long trousers and bicycle clips for many years afterwards.

Albert took great pains to inform Craig and myself that Dram was his arch-enemy. I didn't understand the term though I recalled hearing the same curious term arch from our window cleaner, who described a recent night he had spent with a neighbour, Mrs Clitty. "Big? She was big all right, mate... It was like throwing a marble at Wicker Arch." (Wicker Arch is a railway viaduct in the centre of Sheffield.) What a wonderful analogy! How well we were entertained as children...

Just around the corner from our house was a small wood. Occasionally, we were allowed to visit this mini forest, as it didn't contravene the commandment of not crossing the road. As the Council had run out of tarmac, the road stopped after fifty yards left of our house, and there the wood was situated. On one summer expedition, my friend and I went exploring. Albert was one month older than I was, so he was deemed the leader of our small gang. We meticulously planned our trip:

8:00 a.m.: Set off to woods.
8:03 a.m.: Arrive at woods.
8:04 a.m.: Scout around woods.
8:07 a.m.: Return home.

We were never encouraged to do anything as children so we just made it up as we went along. My family was from poor stock, especially on my Mum's side. They thought that knives and forks were jewellery, and on one of their few visits to Maltby Crags School, they stole the entire collection of cutlery from the dining hall and proudly wore them to Sunday school. Mum's family were entertaining, if not a little interbred.

Grandma was my cousin's dad, but other than my having to sleep with Uncle Jack until the age of twenty-two, they never really bothered us. Uncle Tony was my personal favourite. He lived in White City—a housing development built specifically for the miners who worked at the local colliery and their families— now akin to Beruit! His neighbours the Gannons were school pals of mine. They were a tough family from good stock, and liked by everyone.

Uncle Tony behaved differently, however. He would regularly whip out his catty (catapult) from his Y fronts and carefully load it with a bolly (shiny ball bearing). Subsequently, and for no apparent reason, he would fire it at the house of Mrs Creswell who lived opposite, smashing her windows to pieces. This he did on numerous occasions. He would then motor over to her house, looking all concerned and sympathetic to her predicament, and swear blind that he had witnessed one of the Gannon children committing this thoughtless act. It gave him great pleasure to think he had got the Gannon children into great trouble for crimes they hadn't committed. But that was Tony's sadistic way.

On another occasion, Tony, to his horror, realised that one of the prize cabbages had been stolen from his garden. As an ex-sergeant major, Tony liked everything in order, and the garden was no exception. He regularly inspected his green troops, which all stood perpendicular on his forceful command. He had majestic rows of thirty cabbages, which were as big and as round as a child's head. Uncle T took great pride in his garden, especially in his cabbages. They were like little children to him, along with the other vegetables he had sired. It was blatantly obvious to him that the Gannons had carried out this despicable act of vandalism, and this meant war!

According to Tony, all the world's problems stemmed from the Gannons. It was as simple as that. He blamed this particular family for all global conflict. In his small world, the Gannons were mixed up in terrorism and crime. In reality, the only thing mixed up was Tony's mind!

Battle plans were drawn up and executed with ruthless precision. With the help of his youngest son, Colin, Uncle Tony proceeded to dig a huge hole where the missing prize had been growing. This wasn't any normal-sized hole, but one large enough to bury Tony up to his neck so that just his head was showing, between the remaining greenery in the row. From this splendid vantage point, he would stand— as the hole went down nearly six feet—and wait to catch one of the young Gannons when they dared to come back. A great plan of cunning and ingenuity … or was it?

In the early stages all went well. Uncle Tony lowered himself into the cabbage gulf, and Colin swiftly filled it up with the surrounding soil. So far, so good. Tony then instructed his son to keep a lookout from inside the nearby shed. I think it is appropriate to explain here that Tony's shed was where he brewed his *Gargle-Hooch*, an alcoholic beverage that could strip paint, had the bouquet of stale piss, and tasted like *Scrottock's old bollocks*—which conjures up images of treacly-testicles and mucus. It was, however, easy on the palate if you were an alcoholic, or one in the making. Colin, aged six, indeed was— like father, like son. This proved to be a recipe for disaster.

As night fell, Colin got bored and incredibly thirsty, and so he decided to sample some of his father's moonshine. Two enormous mouthfuls later Colin got incredibly pissed. Tony, on the other hand, was as still mentally sharp as a pin—well, one that was up to his eyeballs in heavy soil. Through the cold night air, a soft silence descended onto the vegetable patch. This was abruptly shattered by Colin, now somewhat out of it. He stumbled buffoon-like from his Dad's still, out of his tree and paralytic from the *grog*. He then promptly relieved himself—over his Dad's head.

Admitting that he had stolen the cabbage, he begged for forgiveness, slurring his words. "Sorry Dad, it was the Gannons. They captured and tortured me and made me do it."

Now this is not the way I would have apologised, but hey, each to his own. When you're only six years young and pissed as a fart, owning up to the crime takes some bottle. Several years passed before I saw Colin again, but when I did bump into him, I was extremely impressed with his wheelchair. Colin went on to become a raging alcoholic, and I'm sad to say, died young.

A son can gravitate towards the familiar behaviour of his father, but why a person becomes a drunk is anyone's guess. It's my opinion that people who are dependent on drink can't help it. It's a disease that the sufferer cannot control. The only way out of this terrible addiction is to stop drinking altogether (easier said than done). Alcohol addiction is like any drug addiction. Deadly! Just one puff on a cigarette can make some people instant addicts. Our local priest once informed me that when he first tried crack cocaine in the back of his vestry, he was instantly hooked.

Chapter 2

Shop Till You're Caught

Like most men, the thought of general shopping is as painful for me as having large pointy needles stuck into my eyes. As a child it was even worse, especially when my Mum insisted we all went as a family to the Maltby market.

By the age of seven, we had moved to Portland Place to share a house with Nan and Grandad. In the grand scheme of things my mother had given birth to a baby girl called Doris, presumably named after our neighbour's dog. Because Mother was of ample proportions, Craig and I never realized she was pregnant. We just thought that she was being crafty as she scooped bigger shares of the family rations, while we resembled albino Biafran children. I think we were unwittingly assumed to have childhood anorexia, but back in those days people thought this normal. As our family had increased, we had no choice but to move to a larger house, literally overnight. We walked approximately one mile to Nan's with all our personal possessions, mine in my school satchel.

Nan and Grandad lived in a three-bedroom house in a more affluent area of Maltby. Here, all the cats still had their tails and didn't have to wear crash helmets, and there was no white coloured dog poo on the streets. I do miss white dog shit and often wonder whatever happened to it.

Life was definitely on the up, and food had now progressed to *pobs*, which was a mixture of warm milk, bread, and sugar. In addition, we now had the luxury of a bath. We would take a real bath once a fortnight, whether we needed one or not. To save hot water and money, Nan would bathe Craig and me, both standing upright in the kitchen sink, with Vim, a household cleaning product, and a scouring pad. To further heap embarrassment on the pair of us, Nan never had any curtains up at the kitchen window, so we would be standing stark naked for all the neighbours to poke fun at. This hideous ritual *eventually* ceased when we reached our respective twenty-first birthdays. As a result Craig hated washing and still has a natural aversion to water and soap. He has perfected the art of the "cat-lick" to three seconds and now has a bath every third week, just so he doesn't get out of the habit. The tide marks he leaves around the bath tub are so thick you can use them as handles to get out with.

Throughout my life, I have always had a fascination with food, which I'm sure stems from my starved upbringing. New foods introduced to us whilst living with Nan included grapes, and tripe coated in vinegar. Without the vinegar, tripe is tasteless. The white, leathery, honeycombed structure was nothing like I'd ever seen or tasted before. When I asked my Nan where tripe came from she curtly explained to me, in her usual acid tone, that Great-Grandma McCloud grew her own tripe up her front passage and vintage grapes up her back passage. I went up and down these passages loads of times and never noticed a thing! Grown-ups' lies and sarcasm are swallowed by their children, and children believe everything they say. With these sorts of fabrications, what chance did I have?

Getting back to our legendary shopping jaunts, on one occasion, we were dragged into the village, like little apprentice Fagins, to the weekly market to peruse the shoddy goods on sale and siphon off a bit of booty. Like most children, we would have been happy to pilfer a pocketful of *scoffs* (sweets)—something small that you would enjoy and easily slip into your front pocket. My mother, however, had different ideas. She would insist we concentrate on more bulky items like turnips, cauliflowers, and especially five-pound bags of spuds.

Being small, scrawny kids, and taking into account the hot weather at the time of the visit, Craig and I must have looked ridiculous in our oversized *Donkey* jackets borrowed from cousin Horace, who was well over six feet tall and twenty-three stone. The jackets in question certainly allowed us to conceal our illicit gains, but due to their size and considerable weight, were complete bastards when we made our getaways. It would have been easier running away in a metal diving suit! The thing that surprises me the most is the fact that we never got caught. I think the stall-holders knew what we were doing, but just felt sorry for us.

The only shop I *did* enjoy going to was a general store called Milnes. This was an emporium of treasure—an Aladdin's cave of riches. I loved this store so much that out of respect, I would only ever steal twelve items per visit. Going to Milnes was a special treat, and one we would all look forward to with relish. Prior to Mother's Day and family birthdays, we were allowed to frequent this store to cast an eye over the presents we were destined to pilfer...

The thing that most vividly sticks in my mind was the toy section at the back of the premises. Here, I would stand in complete awe and bewilderment at the Action Man dolls, wearing different uniforms varying from commandos to skin divers. We could never afford the Action Man figures, but in its infinite wisdom, Milnes had a cheaper version called *Johnny Goes To War*. The quality was significantly inferior to the Action Man doll, and they didn't have the definitive scars on their left cheeks. Action Man was the modern day Rambo. Johnny, on the other hand, was on a par with Prince Edward. I always wanted a scar like the ones Action Man figures so masculinely displayed, and on one occasion, I created a beauty myself, on the right-hand side of my cheek—to appear tough.

Fortunately (or unfortunately for me), whilst stealing a few of Uncle Tony's goosegogs from his beloved allotment, I was caught red-handed by the great man himself. By chance his aim with a sharp Bowie knife was somewhat off the mark that day and luckily only lacerated my earlobe. Uncle T did apologise afterwards, explaining that the particular bottle of hooch he had consumed the previous night was like rocket fuel and caused temporary insanity and blurred vision. Whilst I was in hospital having my ear stitched back together, he did bring me a half-drunk bottle of Lucozade, which was a great show of affection. Whenever I took the orange cellophane wrapper off the Lucozade bottle and held it tight to my face, the world always seemed to look and feel a happier place. I think all people who suffer from the SAD (Seasonal Affective Disorder) syndrome should be encouraged to look at the world through orange glasses or orange cellophane.

As I end this chapter, I am delighted to hear that the makers of Action Man have recently enjoyed record sales. Action Man was launched in Britain in 1966, but was scrapped twenty-two years later. It is making a magnificent resurgence, sporting 1970s football kits now, which is great news for me.

Chapter 3

What's in a Name?

Nowadays, everyone is referred to by his or her proper name. When I was growing up we had nicknames. These titles gave a boy standing within his peer group. Even my own close family and friends still call me by my nickname. I laugh when I hear Wayne Rooney being called "Wassa" by his teammates. When I was growing up, *wassa* was something that came out of your nob!

I had a solid set of mates by the time I was eight years old. Webbo, Ginner, and Bones were my comrades in arms. We were a real gang. The truth be known, we even had intimate knowledge of each other's farting prowess and genitals. We built dens, constructed racing trolleys, fought battles with rival girl gangs, and put dog shit through letter boxes—we were the mutt's nuts!

After school, we would meet up and smoke *bombie-ruffs*, a type of homemade cigarette that was rolled and constructed from the plant we called Mother Die. We used to cut off a six-inch section with our mother of pearl handled pen knives purchased during seaside club trips, and dry it out over a fire to clear it of any earwigs. We would then proceed to stuff it with dried dead leaves and old newspaper. Then we would light up, inhale, cough, and throw up—always in that order. It never did me any harm, and I've managed to get by on only one lung for well over forty years now!

We also liked to play games like *Tin Can Alley, Tiggy-nob, Bloko Bloko 1-2-3,* and *Chicken*. I can count the times I played *Chicken* on one finger. The idea was for all the gang to form a tight circle together facing inwards. We would put our right foot forward and touch everyone else's feet to form an inner circle. The head of the gang, Ginner, would then hold up a large brick, often referred to as a *Charlie*, and drop it downwards onto the unsuspecting toes. The last person to move his foot won the game. I won my very first and last game—and subsequently broke four toes—but I did win! All the team hollered and cheered, and for once, I felt that I'd achieved something with my life. I was so happy I crawled all the way home, desperate to share my accomplishment with Grandad. Looking back now, I realise at that time of my life my IQ was three less than that of a carrot—but *hey ho*—that was then. People barely notice the injury nowadays, though it still causes me to walk rather awkwardly.

My mates expanded tenfold (one new mate per calendar year) by my tenth birthday. And I was beginning to develop a personality, if not a little slowly.

Getting back to nicknames, when you were given a pseudonym, you were a somebody, a character. My pals were mini men with names like Yam, Smig, Spadge, Chalkey, Scone, Chivs, and Poltergeist. You could earn a nickname for your appearance or you could be given one for your talents. Either way, when you got one, it was a badge of honour. We used to have a friend nicknamed "Pumpkin" who was so hideous in the facial department that he was only allowed out on Halloween night.

I honestly feel that the world is desperately short of characters, and that kids today are being morphed into robots with one-syllable words and no spirit or identity—empty shells that are programmed to inflict pain and suffering on others, but not on themselves. I know that not all kids fall into this category, but the majority do because they have lost their sense of worth, moral duty, and values. They are not part of a community and feel alienated and scared. I think the answer is to help them find an identity.

Grandad's era was in a league of its own when it came to nicknames. He had friends with fantastic titles like "Nickie Bozzeye", "Lottie Cockerel", "Granny-green socks", and "Chisel Chin". A particular favourite at the time was "Gypsy Mallet", whose name when mentioned was always followed by "fell off her ladders and broke her leg." These little gems don't crop up in conversation anymore, and it's such a shame. My brother's all-time favourites *are* "Gravy Eyes" and "Bollock Nose", but our local priest took great umbrage to both of these monikers. Grandad also called his mate Stan, who skived off work "Daisies". When I asked him why, he said it was because some days he worked, and some days he didn't!

Later on in my life, I had two great mates whose parents changed their names for different reasons. When I was in the top class at primary school, I made friends with a boy named Joe Carr. In her wisdom, his Mum had his name changed by deed poll to Joe Kerr, which I thought at the time was really cool, because all the kids called him "Joke*r*". I became great mates with another boy named Carl Shore. *Nothing strange about that name*, I hear you saying to yourself, and on first hearing it, I felt the same.

29

One day, he was visiting the doctor's surgery with his dad when the receptionist called out his name. This she did very loudly for the benefit of the other patients who were also sitting in the waiting area. "Is there a C Shore out there?" she laughingly asked.

Well, not to be beaten, Chalkey (Shore-key, as he later came to be known) had his first name changed to begin with a kicking *K*, as opposed to a curly *C*.

One evening, Grandad decided to take me to visit Joey Tickle, one of his mates. On leaving the house, Nan shouted out that we were in for some scattered showers and to dress accordingly. When we arrived at Joey's, his wife informed us that he had gone out for the evening, but asked us in for a brew anyway. As we entered the kitchen, I was startled by the appearance of their eldest son, whose eyes were so far apart it looked as though they were on the sides of his head.

The wife turned to the son and said, "Don't be rude, Cod. Go and fetch some tea for our guests."

"It's all right, Tess, we can't stop," Grandad said, biting his lip to suppress his laughter. "We just wanted to drop off this book for Joey and, by the look of this weather, we'd better be making tracks. We've not got our coats, and it's lagging it down now."

Making a hasty retreat, we stepped back into a storm, bid Tess Tickle farewell, and subsequently got drenched right through.

Arriving home, Grandad turned to me and said, "Scattered fucking showers my arse."

"Who said that?" Nan screeched out angrily.

"Noah," Grandad replied.

Chapter 4

Swimming at the Lido with Bazza

When you reached the age of eight, it was fashionable to be seen down the Crags, common land surrounded on one side by outcrops of magnesium limestone and a stream, or *dyke* as we used to refer to it, on the other. Adjacent to the dyke at the lower end of the Crags sat a small, open air swimming pool aptly named Maltby Baths, which is pretty much what it was used for by the residents of Maltby, myself included. The water was relatively clean and had little coal residue, which was good enough for me. The strong chemicals in the water could also strip away any amount of grime you had built up on your person.

Maltby Baths, or the lido, as it was occasionally referred to, was run by an old couple named Mini and Sid. They were later to achieve cult status, for reasons unknown to most. Sid was your typical sergeant major, and Mini was Eastern European. They were great characters who were loved and respected by all the residents of Maltby. Everyone learned to swim with Mini and Sid, even Tarzan and Captain Webb. Their technique was pretty straightforward, if not a little unorthodox. You would turn up at the lido freezing cold—even at the height of summer—and terrified of the prospect of getting even colder when you entered the water. I swear that the water in the lido was directly fed from the abutting brook, but mixed with liquid nitrogen for added freeze factor.

31

The instant the water lapped over your feet at the shallow end, your testicles embarked on a journey northwards to link up with your Adam's apple.

Mini would line all the non-swimmers up and bark out her instructions. First, she would reassure us that all the floating insects on the pool surface were dead or dying so we just had to ignore them. (To this day, some of the species in that pool have still not been identified.) Second, she would smile and order us all to dive in head first. (What part of not being able to swim did she not understand? I've never met anyone that could dive before they could swim.) On top of that, we were all standing in the foot pool, ten feet away from the pool itself and only two inches deep!

When we did finally get into the water, Mini produced a large pole with a sharp barbed hook on the end. Sid told us it was used by Captain Ahab when he was out hunting Moby Dick on his ship, *Pequod*. (It's funny to look back now and think that when I was a child, I believed everything grown-ups told me without question.)

Mini would yell out some instructions in a mixture of Eastern European and Yorkshire, with a few choice expletives thrown in for good measure, and then slowly move the skewering end of the pole towards us. This combination could have stopped Hitler in 1939! You were safer nearer the pool side due to the pole being twelve feet long, but the poor buggers who were in the middle would scramble frantically through the water, desperately trying to avoid being harpooned. Taking into account the dreaded barb on the end of the pole, when she said "swim," you swam—in whatever fashion you could, forgetting about the fact that the further you went the deeper the water got. Nobody gave a hoot about drowning or sinking—we just doggie paddled our way to the other end to escape Mini's spear. It was effective, though. We all learned to swim on our first lesson, even if the lesson lasted four days.

On one visit to the baths, I bumped into a boy called Bazza, who just happened to be a little bit stupid, making me look and sound extremely intelligent. Bazza was depriving a village of its idiot, and the only big word he ever knew was *wheelbarrow*. I don't want to sound too harsh about Bazza's lack of intelligence, but I'm sorry to say, he was as thick as shit and knew it. You'd say "Good morning" to Baz, and he'd be stuck for an answer. Bazza's reply to any question was "Chips," no matter what the question was. From an early age, Baz spent his time "spanking his monkey" (masturbating), which constantly gave him enormous pleasure. Apparently, he was permanently jacked up on an early herbal form of Viagra, which his Aunty Mary put in his tea. He was also hung like a baboon and had a beard, but he assured us he was only ten years old, and that was good enough for me.

Baz suggested we get changed together in the same cubicle, and normally I wouldn't have hesitated (Laurel and Hardy did it all the time), but that day something was different. Something didn't feel or look right. I managed to notice that he had brought what I thought were his sandwiches with him and stuffed them in the front of his undies. It *did* seem quite odd at the time so I declined his request. This huge bulge in his *kecks*, or swimming trunks, resembled a tube so maybe he was going to have sausage rolls for lunch. But I never found out.

After what seemed like a lifetime, Baz strutted towards the deep end of the pool with a big smirk across his face. As he approached the water, I can only describe what I saw as *gi-fucking-gantic*. Whatever he had down his trunks needed a license. It should have been fed buns. At that age, I had no idea it was just his tadger. I thought he had smuggled his brother into the lido down his trunks. Mini caught sight of Baz and his hidden anaconda, and promptly poked it hard with her pointy stick. What happened next was fantastic. The barb on the end of the pole caught hold of Bazza's trunks, and when Mini pulled it toward her to attract his attention, his trunks came off. Baz stood there stark bollock naked for everyone and his grandma to see, and what a sight it was. Mini pretended to pass out, but I think she was overcome. Baz, however, proceeded to dive in. You've never seen so many girls go down—under the water that is—in your life. When he surfaced, the first thing to see daylight was his periscope. At this point, Sid had taken to the water and swiftly managed to wrestle Baz and his snake to the poolside. He pulled Baz out by his wanger and barred him for life. Mini was never the same again. I think Mini's shock was her amazement at someone having a bigger weapon (pole) than the one she was bandying around at the time!

When Baz left school, he got a job in a photographic studio called Crimages and became a human tripod. It was said that when he got out of bed in a morning, three things touched the floor first, and neither of these were his legs. The boy/man is a legend in his own lunchtime/lunchbox.

Chapter 5

Dib, Dib, Dib ...
Dob, Dob, Dob

One November evening after school, Mother proudly announced to the family that I was to join the Cub Scouts. No discussion or questions—she had been given a uniform by her friend, Phoebe, and I was enrolled the same night. The uniform was unbelievably big, but as usual, I had to make do and subsequently became the laughing stock of our street. Grandad said I looked a *Bobbie dazzler*, but the jury was out on his opinion. I actually didn't mind the shirt, but I did object to the long, hooped socks and garters with dangling flags. The neckerchief made me feel like a cowboy, but then Nan told me to remove it from my mouth and wear it properly along with the accompanying matching *woggle*. It felt all wrong, but I didn't have a say in it. There I stood at the front door, looking like a real fashionista in my smart, yet ill-fitting, apparel.

I was cast out into the damp, dreary, autumnal evening like a lamb to the slaughter or a cub to be culled. Being dressed for a paedophile's jamboree didn't help. To add further insult, just as I was leaving our house, Mum scooped her hand into a bowl of cold chip fat next to the door and expertly daubed it on my fringe, which was always sticking up at the time. At least it made her feel better. So, adorned with my greasy hair and a half-closed right eye (the lump of lard on this occasion was of gigantic proportion), I set off on my journey, never to return as the same boy. (Now much older, I dream about having a fringe

35

again. I once grew my hair long at the back to create a fringe, when I started losing my lovely locks.)

It was approximately half a mile from our house to the Cub Scout Headquarters and should have taken ten minutes. Armed with in-depth knowledge of other scouts mercilessly persecuted by rival gangs, I decided to give myself half an hour. Within this period, I factored into my plans the possibility of hiding inside several dustbins and running at least fifteen miles away from these bullies, in the complete opposite direction to where I was supposed to be heading. As I turned the corner at the bottom of our street, I was ambushed by twelve big boys and soundly thrashed to within an inch of my life.

To this day, I still cannot fathom who gave these would-be assassins such accurate inside information. (My mother remains a suspect.) Having regained my senses and brushed myself down, I was struggling to breathe because one of the boys had removed my woggle and tied the tightest *granny knot* ever on my neckerchief, obviously wrapped around my neck. Trying to release myself and breathe properly proved fruitless until I remembered that I had my trusted mother of pearl handled pen knife inside my pocket. Within a flash and with the dexterity of Sweeney Todd, I quickly severed the fabric and cut straight into my earlobe. The neckerchief did, however, act as a super bandage, and the grease stemmed the flow of blood. At the sight of my blood and the knife, my attackers quickly pissed off.

You would think that having gone through this amount of trauma in such a short time and being so close to home, I would have made a speedy retreat to the sanctuary of our house. No way! I was made of sterner stuff. In truth, the only reason I didn't go home was because I imagined my mother kicking the shit out of me for ruining my uniform. I managed to hobble to the bottom of the cinder path, which ended outside the local police station where I could seek some kind of relative safety. From there I saw the scout hut and decided to take a breather and collect my thoughts. Just when I thought it couldn't get any worse, God decided to piss on my chips—four twelve-year-olds from a rival gang happened to be hiding behind the wall of the station. They pounced on me with lightning speed, grabbing my arms and throat.

Whilst simultaneously pissing down my legs, I shouted out as loud as I could muster, *"Hands up for a policeman!"*

In days gone by, everyone, especially children, respected the law. When a policeman told you off, you were terrified, not only for the official bollocking from the copper, but for the impending beating you'd get when your parents found out about it. When you cried out, "Hands up for a policeman," kids did just that. They stopped what they were doing and put their hands up into the air. As luck would have it, my assailants did what I asked. Bloody marvellous, it worked! I didn't hang around to stop and discuss my actions. I just legged it to the hut.

When I got into my early teens, my mate Lofty and I were apprehended by a policeman named P.C. Pilsbury for lobbing empty milk bottles at a group of middle-aged Morris dancers. If you committed this serious crime nowadays, you would be taken to a station and given access to three lawyers, two social workers, and a barrister. You would then be asked to attend a seminar on moral values and furnished with a huge cheque for not pressing charges against the Morris dancers for having bells on their knackers and wearing loud shirts in a built-up area.

In the society we now live in, we reward wrong-doers and penalise the law-abiding citizens. We accept lying, cheating politicians who thrive on spin, ignore global warming, nurture failing educational standards, put up with dirty hospitals, and tolerate serious rising crime. We are obsessed with statistics and moving targets and have lost a true sense of national pride.

In the early 60s, however, things were a little different. The bobby, or policeman in question, just walloped you on the side of your head. We used to refer to this as a "thick ear". This happened to me once, and even though I developed a nasty twitch and have been profoundly deaf ever since, it certainly taught me a lesson. Whenever I bump into P.C. Pilsbury, I thank him for showing me the error of my ways and putting me back on the straight and narrow. He alone woke me up to face moral and social issues with dignity and a sense of worth. How ironic is that?

At last, I arrived at my destination—a little shell-shocked, but in one piece. I was greeted at the door by the scout leader, officially known as *Akala*, which according to Grandad, roughly translated means "kiddie feeler". Fortunately for us, our leader was a smashing guy and hated kids. He was also a touch eccentric.

He took one look at me and bellowed out, "What the chuffing hell is that boys?"

During my lifetime I have been made to feel more welcome. But looking back and realising what kind of state I was in, you couldn't blame the scout master for his remarks. One boy did vaguely recognise me though, so I was reluctantly accepted into the group.

Akala instructed all the leaders, who were referred to as *Sixers*, to get their patrols to line up in an orderly fashion at the front of the hut. I was accepted in the Beaver pack, due to the fact it only had two other people in it, not six like the others. I discovered that every pack had a leader and an assistant, referred to as a *Seconder*, and four slaves. I became the Beaver slave boy in less than five minutes.

When some order and decorum had been restored, our grand leader commanded us to begin the activity, which on this particular night would be knots and lashings. Less than ten minutes earlier, I'd been lashed senseless by a bunch of crazed psychos and knotted around the throat with my neckerchief until I nearly died. What was he thinking?

Bugger that for a game of soldiers, I thought. *Just how much abuse can a lad take in one day?* My expression must have said it all because all the others turned to me with sympathetic frowns. Wisely, Akala then opted for something a little more interesting— whittling a tent peg out of wood using pen knives. All boys carried knives in those days, but for the right reasons.

The two boys in my section were Domino and Plug. Domino was a nice boy—nice and fat. His arse had two post codes. When he got older, he had his ear pierced and gravy came out. I was a little jealous of Domino because of how he had acquired such a bulk and how much food he must have had to eat to get so rotund. He had a face within a face and reminded me of Oliver Hardy. Domino was not remotely funny though and bone bloody idle. I saw him exercising once—one, two, three and then the other eyelid. When he got baptised, the priest used Lake Windermere. Even his belly button made an echo.

Plug, on the other hand, was totally different. Plug was short for *plug ugly*. This lad wasn't ugly— he abused the privilege. His mother used to feed him with a catapult. His father would tie a piece of meat around his neck just so the dog would play with him. Plug had a face that resembled a blistered piss pot. He was so laid back he was horizontal. Life had dealt him a shit hand when it came to looks. But beauty, as they say, is only skin deep. Well, if that really was the case, Plug was born inside out. Plug just got on with getting on. He didn't say much, just smiled. I really liked him—a nice lad. The only problem with Plug was Domino, and how these guys got put together, I will never know. They were total opposites in every sense of the word. Domino would bark out instructions to Plug, and Plug would gesture to the *lard arse* where to go and shove his head.

Akala had to go to the toilet during our tent peg session so the cubs were left to their own devices for two hours. Domino decided that we should have a quick game of Stretch, where you stand opposite a partner at a distance of three feet with your legs together. Then one person throws a knife to either side of the opposition's feet, and the knife must stick in the ground. The fact we were playing in a wooden hut was ideal. If and when the knife sticks in the floor, the other player has to stretch one of his feet out to where the knife lands. To break the stretch and get your feet back together, you have to throw the knife directly between your partner's feet and make it stick again. The whole point of the game is to display just how good you are at throwing a knife and how far you can part your legs without falling over. Domino and Plug took up their respective positions. Plug threw first, and firmly and adeptly embedded the knife in Domino's big toe. *Game over*. Utter shock and terror descended on the spectators. You could have cut the atmosphere with a knife—or a toe, perhaps? I went home that night in a daze, wondering just what I'd let myself in for.

Chapter 6
The Club Trip

Once every year courtesy of the local working men's club, all the local kids would be taken on a trip to the seaside for the day. Ours was referred to affectionately as the "Slip trip". (The term *slip* was used by the miners from the local colliery, who used to slip into the club on the way home from their shift at the pit to sink a few sherbets. My Grandads kept this establishment going for many years due to them both having a thirst like a dredger.)

When I was eight years old, the trip that particular year was to Cleethorpes, or *Clathapees*, as we would call it, due to our limited intelligence and lack of verbal dexterity. At 6:00 a.m. on an August morning, Craig and I met up with our buddies Titch, Pipes, and Domino outside the club, extremely boisterous and excited. Our transport wasn't expected to arrive until 7:00 a.m., but we had plans to make and things to do. Typical English summer weather proved to be on the cards for the day—it was drizzling fine rain. This did not dampen our spirits though, and the first item on the day's agenda was what type of pen knife we were going to buy when we arrived. Every year, the club's organiser gave each child a goody bag and fifty pence to spend on whatever they wanted. No thought or question came into our minds over what to spend such a huge amount of *spendulics*, or money, on—it was always a penknife.

After standing around for thirty minutes in the damp atmosphere, each child getting progressively louder by the second and fighting for air space, the conversation came to an abrupt halt when Domino spewed up all the morning's offerings he had previously rammed down his cake-hole, over the back of Titch's head. Without any warning, this projectile vomit came out at the speed of sound and turned Titch's bonse into a technicolour pizza helmet. We all stood back in horror when Domino told us he was sorry, but had now made some more room for his other *scran* and proceeded to eat another sandwich without breaking sweat. Titch became all tearful, which in the current circumstances, he had every right to do. Then Pipes scolded him for attention-seeking and being a *mardy* (someone who whines and moans a lot). This poor lad was about to spend the day at the seaside attired in second-hand puke, which he didn't ask for, and I'm pretty sure, didn't want. Titch was also warned by Domino not to *sprag*, or inform on him, and made him promise to say a passing bird had done it. Some big bloody bird that must have been!

The coach arrived on time, and we all scrambled on, kicking and shoving the smaller kids out of the way as we headed straight for the back seat. This seat was reserved for the tough kids, who were held in high regard by all the other children. We managed to stay on the seat for about thirty seconds, until a group of bigger lads, led by a notorious bully who went by the name of *Fat Owl*, dragged us off one by one, twisting our ears in the process and following up with a swift kick up the arse. We re-formed ourselves into our tight gang of five and decided to sit nearer the front of the coach, closer to the driver and club's representative.

A small, geeky-looking lad, adorned with two identical barrels of snot dangling from his nostrils,

sat next to us and wisely suggested, as an act of retribution, we spit on the bullies' sandwiches before they
were handed out to them. All the kids' rations for the
day were perched on the seat in front of us. All we
had to do was open a few up on the top of the pile,
leave our ghastly deposits on them, carefully replace
them, and … *Bob's your uncle, Fanny's your aunt*. The
helper on the bus always handed the sandwiches out
starting from the back and working forwards. It was
a little treat for us all and made up for the fact that
most of the children wouldn't have had any breakfast that particular morning. To our surprise, Pipes
had brought along a small tub of grease which would
further enhance our devious plot. He suggested this
would be tastier, but after consultation, we decided to
put both on. We may have been ousted from our rear
throne, but every dog has its day, and this day would
be ours. Better still, no one would even suspect us of
this dirty, devilish deed.

Quick as a flash, the top four packages were
adeptly prised open from the nearby box, and the
greasy gross mixture was added to the stale *potted dog*
spread already on the bread –plan expertly executed
with military precision. All we had to do now was
patiently wait until we reached the halfway point of
the journey. The sandwiches would then be dispensed.
The pent up excitement was killing us—so much so
that Titch said he *had a little fat lad on*, meaning he
was somewhat aroused down in the nether regions
of his hairy banana. The bus was nearing the turnoff,
for a toilet stop, followed by the veritable feast of
potted meat sarnies. All the kids disembarked and
raced frantically to the loos to relieve their bladders,
in some cases as big as the bus itself.

No thought of washing their little hands, the
kids raced back to their seats, eagerly awaiting their

44

refreshments. To our horror, the coach driver and his helper were bent-up double in the car park, throwing up from their toe ends. The overall sight and sound was frightening. Vomit everywhere—all the way down the steps of the coach, on the driver's seat, on the front of the bus—pretty much all over the place. The two men were in a terrible state, screaming at each other in foreign tongues and expletives, each punctuated with more hurls of sick. Obviously the two men had helped themselves to the first few packages on top of the pile, and without question, wolfed them down at great speed, not realising the hidden surprise awaiting their taste buds. The expression Granny used to use in situations similar to these was "Holy shit," and I must admit my arse was going sixpence, shilling… at the thought of being rumbled.

During the complete melee, we gingerly got back into our respective seats and pretended to be tired and nod off. What seemed like an age went by. Then, finally, with a reserve driver having to take the wheel, we set off again with none of the children on board having anything at all to eat. All the remaining sandwiches were condemned for fear of further food poisoning. The plan had spectacularly failed to hit the target, but at least we had not been caught out. Nobody was any the wiser, and the four-eyed geek who planted the seeds of devastation was sworn to secrecy by a little death threat, which did seem to have the desired effect.

We finally pulled up to the coach station, somewhat relieved and excited at the prospect of not getting caught for our major prank, and not actually killing anyone. Any remorse we might have felt had been quickly replaced by the tantalising prospect of procuring a new blade. With lightning speed, we headed like an Exocet missile to Arnie's Daggers and Swords, which was a weapons armoury situated near the station. Within minutes, we were equipped with our new knives, happy in the knowledge that we had spent all our money in one go. The prospect we now faced was having to kill another six hours of mindless roaming around nameless streets in pissing down rain, starving hungry due to the fact that a few bleeding idiots had interfered with the sandwiches. The word that springs to mind is *priceless*! But we were Maltby kids, and a little hunger and a bit of rain wouldn't hurt us or spoil our day. We were made of sterner stuff. We were not nesh (cold). Truth be known, I was so starving at the time I would have gladly eaten pig's dick and lettuce followed by a large portion of shit with sugar on it.

Chapter 7

Mischievous Night

Apart from Christmas Eve, my favourite night of the year was the 4th of November—known as Mischievous Night, and the evening before Bonfire Night, or *Bommy Night*. I loved this special occasion because it was the only time of the year that parents turned a blind eye to their children's behaviour. You could get away with naughty deeds and really piss off your neighbour for the best part of the evening, and pretty much everyone accepted it in the spirit it was meant— bad. It was a Northern tradition, steeped in history and passed down from generation to generation—a night of mischief in every sense of the word.

After tea, Ginner and Webbo called for me to discuss final plans and arrangements for the forth- coming night's activities. It was forever a source of amusement when Ginner came by.

He always whispered to me, "Have you got any matches?"

If he asked me this once, he asked a million times, and the answer was always the same, "No!" Why he wanted matches every time he popped around to see me, I never found out. Maybe he was a secret twisted fire starter or maybe he liked the smell of sulphur when he ignited his farts.

We decided to begin our pranks on the next street, to deflect attention from our immediate families and closest neighbours. Though every other kid did this so the effort was futile.

Firstly, we would pay Mr Dickman a visit, due to the fact he was a complete arsehole. Dickman by name—*dick man* by nature. Old Dickie hated all things, including people, animals, and the weather. It was rumoured that he didn't even like himself. He spent his days constantly complaining to parents about the lack of respect, dearth of manners, and scarcity of discipline in society in general. The man was in a league of his own for whinging. Nothing was right with the world, and he didn't have a good word for anyone. Grandad called him "an arse dribble."

We decided to leave a large dollop of dog shit outside his front door, cover it with newspaper, set it alight, knock on the door and then run off. He in turn would answer the door, see the paper on fire, and quickly stamp it out with the bedroom slippers he always wore. The end result would be Dickie extinguishing the flames, and in the process, getting his slippers covered in sloppy dog doo. Ginner said it would be "a piece of piss."

All went to plan, right up to Dickie putting out the flames, but a piece of burning newspaper floated upwards, setting fire to the dangling cord holding up his pyjamas. Bloody bedlam ensued. Webbo took matters into his own hands, leapt out from a nearby hedge, whipped out his dangleberry, and proceeded to piss on Mr Dickman to extinguish the flames.

In hindsight, I think the plan was ill-thought out, but credit goes to Webbo for sheer nerve and courage under fire, so to speak. The look on Dickie's face was one of sheer horror. He contorted and writhed in agony, and Mr Dickman nearly became Mr Dickless. It was only the mouldy, matured, homemade gorgonzola that he was cultivating in his undercrackers that helped stem the spread of flames—coupled, of course, with Webbo's urine. Webbo made a hasty getaway and disappared into the night. If Mr Dick-man had captured Webbo, I'm sure he'd have nailed his knackers to the floorboards.

Our next port of call that evening was a friend of Mr Dickman's—another old git affectionately known as Crumpleforeskin. This chap was so old he could remember the Dead Sea when it was alive. He was a cantankerous relic who took great pleasure in being nasty to everyone. He was also the meanest man in Maltby. Grandad said he used to turn the gas off when he turned his toast over. He once suffered a heart attack, when he threw a penny to some begging orphans and the string snapped. This guy was high on our hit list.

As we made our way stealthily through the back gardens of Norfolk Place hedge-hopping with a spring in our step, I noticed three boys from a rival gang hidden nearby. I immediately notified my mates, and we concealed ourselves behind an old coal house. Through the murky smoke-filled night, we observed the three lads lying flat to the floor, their breath visible in short, fast, rhythmic chugs like that of a steam engine. These boys had just carried out an identical trick to the one we had done at old Dickie's. From our vantage point, we saw a strapping man barge out through his front door, missing the ignited paper as he went, bellowing at the top of his voice what he was going to shove up the culprits' arseholes when he caught them.

Not being too friendly with our rival gang, I picked up a large wall brick, lying idly at the side of our hideout, and with the precision of David (as in David and Goliath), majestically hurled the brick through the night sky towards the three stooges. With bang on accuracy, the projectile landed with an almighty thud just inches from where they were camped. All three boys leapt to their feet, screaming at the top of their voices, allowing the enraged gentleman to pinpoint their position. With the grace and speed of a marauding elephant, the guy in question apprehended all the boys and soundly thrashed each and every one of them. Like sly foxes, we vanished into the darkness, pissing our sides.

It's strange to think that nowadays you cannot raise an eyebrow to a child without getting arrested. When I was a lad, my mother would regularly belt Craig and me to keep us in check. If you got the cane at school for being naughty, you would shit yourself all the way home because when your parents found out, you were punished all over again—only this time it was much harder.

Mum would clip us around the back of the head and say, "That's for what you think you got away with."

On another occasion, she excelled herself in Blackham's supermarket and invented her own style of punishment. I was tormenting Craig, which was, and still is my favourite pastime. Mum turned, gripped my left shoulder with her left hand, and proceeded to whack me around the head with the palm of her right hand. As she doled out the punishment, she spun me around at the same time. Every word she uttered was followed by a *crack* on the skull, and in turn, by a full bloody spin.

"You..." (smack, full body rotation) "little..." (smack, full body rotation) "bleeder..."

I must say that this kind of punishment never did me any lasting damage, apart from the constant nosebleeds, motion sickness, and incessant blinking. Oh, and the Tourettes!

Seeing our adversaries being clobbered by the big bloke certainly put us all on a high. Crumpleforeskin was in for a ride. Catlike, we made our way over a rickety fence that surrounded our victim's garden, and without a sound, continued through his vegetable patch. At last, we reached a vantage point that enabled us to survey the terrain, and more importantly, spot the whereabouts of Crumple. Normally, he was waiting by his external coal bunker, but on this specific night, he was nowhere to be seen. Crumple had been a target for kids like us every Mischievous Night, so in his old and positively ancient age, the wizened gnome had become a lot wiser and had taken to hiding out. This made the game even better, but instilled in us all a misplaced confidence. Having failed to locate our intended victim or give the guy any credit for counter planning, we cautiously strolled down the cinder path, which led straight to Crumple's back door.

Ginner removed the rotten eggs he had been transporting and gently placed the smelly missiles into each gang member's hand. The plan was to run up a strategically placed plank of wood, which led onto a coal bunker situated approximately six feet from our victim's rear door. Having reached the summit of the bunker, the idea was to lob the stink bomb and hit above the door just as Crumple answered it. The rotten mess would then fall onto his head and face. My job was to knock on the door and raise the attention of said occupant. It needed precise timing. During our surveillance we had not spied the enemy, so things looked pretty good. On the command of "Foggy, seggy, laggy," (First, second, last), I would rattle the door knocker, and the squadron of stink bombers would take off, dropping their payloads directly on the target at tremendous speed. Due to the fact each of us had two bombs, we hoped the chance of hitting the target, or even Crumple as he answered the door, would be pretty high. As well as attracting

Crumple's interest, I also had to make my way up the plank, onto the bunker, and release my shells. Being the rear gunner placed me in a precarious position, but as I was the smallest on this particular mission, it was my turn.

A deathly silence fell over the area, now covered in a cloud of thick black smoke drifting over from a neighbour's garden, making finding the actual position of my comrades extremely difficult. Through the still night air, I distinctly heard the words: "Foggy, seggy, laggy." What I didn't realise at the time was that the instructions came from Crumple, who had hidden inside the coal bunker. (Clever bastard.) Ginner set off like a meatloaf, or a bat out of hell, and hit the plank at speeds nearing Mach 2. The instant his front foot hit the timber, it broke clean in two. (Prior to our visit, Crumple had cleverly sawed through the wood, until it only just stayed in one piece.) The plank cracked, piercing the night like a strangled cat, and Ginner bellowed out a cry of anguish as he smashed into the rear of the concrete bunker. To make things worse, Webbo landed directly on top of him, causing Ginner to yell out even louder the second time. Both boys lay there, yelping in pain, covered in rotten eggs. Crumple appeared from his bunker, and stood *Churchillian* over his captors. Victory was his—or so he thought; what he had failed to take into account was me.

Having observed the fiasco from several yards away and monitoring events as they happened, gave me the advantage of summarising the entire operation and making a monumental decision. I decided to give Crumple a surprise egg shampoo. Quick as a flash and with the touch of a midwife, I pounced from behind him and delivered my cargo onto the top of his scalp, catching him completely by surprise.

Crumple crumpled before my very eyes, and I hastily grabbed my mates and forcibly dragged them to the safety of the large privet hedge beside the coal bunker. Pulling them through it proved somewhat difficult, but when adrenalin begins to turn brown, you always seem to cope.

Chapter 8

Bommy Wooding

Following the previous eventful night's entertainment, normality prevailed somewhat on the next day. Bonfire Night, or *Bommy Night*, as it was referred to in the north of England, on the 5th of November.

During the weeks leading up to this day, all the gangs throughout the neighbourhood busily collected firewood from the outlying forests and surrounding woodlands. Little kids with blackened brows and grime-encrusted hands were hard at work felling trees and chopping up dead branches so their loot would be small enough to drag home to their respective timber stores, ready for the big night. Kids would think nothing of travelling five or six miles to axe limbs from trees and rip up old fence posts for their collections. Not a thought or care in the world was spared for the hundreds of cows and sheep they liberated in the quest for collecting timber. The only thing that mattered to "Freedom Firemen" was the size of the fire.

Today, this would be construed as a blatant act of vandalism. But on the plus side, children were getting out in the fresh air and exercising their legs and arms, if not their axe skills. Walking down the road, armed with a pickaxe and several cleavers, might appear somewhat threatening to the casual passerby. But in my youth, these murder weapons were only used for the task in hand—cutting timber.

The target destination for our timber supplies was situated on the lower slopes of the slag heaps encircling the working mine. This was known as the "Pit Woods" and resembled a petrified forest. The trees were bleached and scarred by pollution from the colliery and appeared dead and lifeless to the world. Birds and rabbits inhabited this wasteland, but were thin on the ground because my Uncle Tony constantly stalked the place in search of quarry for supper. The area was snared and gin-trapped like a minefield—and only a few expert woodsmen could roam these grounds safely. Fortunately, I had been schooled in the craft of tracking and trailing, but I still only went to this eerie place once a year in the company of my Uncle Tony.

Uncle T was always the fire master and led our team of young men into the depths of the woods. He carefully selected a dead tree and issued his orders. I desperately longed to point out that all the trees in this particular wood were dead, but held my tongue. To decide who wielded the axe, we went through the ritual of a game called "Paper, Scissors, and Stone". This game has decided world conflicts in the past and was taken very seriously. The contest is played by each opponent putting his right hand behind his back. On the count of three, both players thrust their respective hands forward to meet the other person in the style of one of the chosen formats: paper, depicted by a flat, upright hand; scissors, illustrated by separating the first two fingers on the hand to form a "V" shape; and stone, which takes the form of a clenched fist. The reasoning behind the game is this: paper beats stone because it can wrap around it; stone beats scissors because it can smash it, and scissors beat paper because it can cut through it. In the event of both competitors producing the same hand sign, they call it a tie and draw their hands again. (I think that the government should pass legislation to make this ritual compulsory, whenever politicians reach a stalemate.) There can only be one winner, and even though luck plays a large part, decisions are made and problems resolved.

On this particular day, the outright winner was a boy called Jammy, which is also a northern phrase associated with people who are deemed lucky. Jammy lived near Uncle Tony, who had innocently invited him along for the day. Because he was funny, likable, good-looking, and jammy, the boys and I took an instant dislike to him. On top of that, he was taller than the rest of us, but younger in age. Jammy was good at everything. I bet he could have juggled soot if asked to! Or fall in cow shit and come out smelling of roses. He was the type of boy who I wouldn't have pissed on if he had been on fire. Another way of deciding a leader was a game in which we regularly participated called "Toss you for it, first to fill a thimble". I had no idea how to play it correctly and cannot recall it ever coming to anything.

Jammy felled the mighty tree, and by gum, it came crashing down to earth. With the precision of a well disciplined ant colony, we lashed the fallen tree with a large rope and formed two identical lines parallel to each other. Off we merrily trundled home, heaving the bulky timber behind us. Nobody complained of the strain of dragging such a huge log. We just set our bearings for home and off we went.

Having arrived back at base camp, which in our case was Ginner's back garden, we carefully stacked our prize wood with the rest of our assorted collection. When it came to materials to go onto the fire, we would burn anything we could lay our hands on back then, including old car tyres, discarded carpets, and dead animals—the list was endless. Stacking and guarding our pile was as important to our gang as collecting it. Numerous rival gangs in our neighbourhood wouldn't think twice about stealing our stock. By doing this, it saved them all the time and strain of felling and dragging logs several miles home. Instead, they liked to pilfer it from unsuspecting fellow collectors and move it a few hundred yards into their territory.

We all took it in turns to guard our store and always made sure there were at least two members of our group present—one on lookout patrol and one strategically hidden within the stack. We made our collection into a large den, securing the biggest logs together with rope. It wasn't just any old den—it was a fortress built to withstand all invaders. We took real pride in our camp and guarded it with our lives. We cleverly rigged a trap, not only to repel our enemies, but to injure them in the process.

Late one October evening, three members of a gang led by a nasty lad called Buster decided to pay us a visit. Craig was on sentry duty and spotted them sneaking up the cinder track heading for our lair. He alerted Webbo and me, and we quickly put into place our counterattacking plan.

Our den was six feet high, built in the shape of a square, and backing onto Ginner's outhouse. On the flat top of the outhouse, we had placed several large logs about five feet long and twelve inches across, stacked like a pyramid, four feet to the apex, and approximately twenty pieces of timber. All the logs were tethered together with a loose length of rope, and being sited on the roof, were well off the ground. The rope had been tied in such a way that with a deliberate yank the majority of the logs would roll

57

off the outhouse roof, directly onto the unsuspecting thieves, with dramatic and hopefully, traumatic consequences.

We located our adversaries climbing over the fence. Silence was called for so we reverted to sign language. When you have been part of a close gang, spending lots of quality time together and understanding each other's thoughts and feelings, all it takes for effective communication is a nod or a wink. Buster beckoned to his mates to bend over and place their hands together, interlocking their fingers in order to provide him with a foothold, or a "leg up". Buster then carefully placed his foot into one of the boy's hands and levered himself upwards, using the boy's shoulder and the wall for balance and support. He then raised his opposite foot into the other boy's hand and repeated the procedure until he was semi-suspended by his mates halfway up the wall of the outhouse. Buster was no doubt feeling very smug with himself at this particular moment in time as he neared his goal of stealing our wood. He obviously hadn't factored into his plans our countermeasures. Under his considerable weight, his two comrades didn't quite look so pleased. But they were now within striking distance of their objective.

Alas, that's when their premature joy turned to terror and pain. With one sharp tug of the rope, most of the precariously stacked logs came crashing down onto all three of them, taking Buster's eyebrows clean off in the process. What a top result for our team. Three pathetic stooges lay buried beneath our bommy wood, battered and bruised beyond recognition. However, the noise of the tumbling logs, coupled with the tortured screams of pain from the submerged lads, alerted Ginner's dad, who staggered out of the back door, half pissed from the afternoon drinking session. Tripping over a stray chunk of wood, he landed smack on top of Buster and his henchmen. In the commotion that followed, the gang and I slipped away into the night with the stealth of foxes, inwardly pissing ourselves with both laughter and pride. What a fabulous result.

Another way of warding off rival gangs was to bombard them with flying sparklers, which were known as the "poor man's rocket". Like me, none of my mates had any money. So when it came around to Bonfire Night, we had to make do with watching other people's displays from afar and pretending to send rockets into the cosmos by lobbing lighted sparklers, whilst simultaneously whistling loudly for added effect. It never impressed anyone, especially our parents, who thought it childish and dangerous. I agree it was childish, as we were children at the time. I also concur that it was bloody dangerous, but it was effective at fending off our enemies.

When the big day arrived, all the kids would meet up first thing in the morning and begin to transport all the stored timber and tyres to the bonfire site. This was a waste piece of ground at the side of Nan's house. Parents would gladly join in and contribute to assembling the fire, which could sometimes reach to well over twelve feet high and as many feet across. This was a time of year when people would rid themselves of all their unwanted junk, and all their respective rubbish would be heaped onto the fire. Not a thought was spared for pollution, global warming, exploding aerosol cans, or recycling. People just de-cluttered their houses and sheds of unwanted goods.

Touching on the subject of global warming, the problem with the term is that it sounds so appealing to people who live in the northern half of Britain. It conjures up images of the Mediterranean sun, wall to wall azure-coloured skies, and happiness. I now live in the small village of Whiston in South Yorkshire, which lies in a valley overlooked by Ulley Reservoir. Due to unprecedented summer storms in 2007, the deluge of rain caused the dam to breech, and it nearly burst its banks. Being approximately forty-seven feet deep and covering an area of thirty-three acres, this wall of water could have wiped out several little villages like ours if it wasn't for the excellent efforts of the fire service and other government departments.

Global warming should be renamed "worldwide destruction". Then people might sit up and take it more seriously. The burning of fossil fuels and the emissions of CF gases are destroying the polar ice caps, which are melting. The Gulf Stream then stops protecting us, and the last thing it becomes is warm. On the contrary, we will start to have freezing winters and pissing wet summers. The only winners will be the insurance companies, who will start increasing our premiums—that is, if they will insure us at all!

On the theme of recycling, my children think it doesn't affect or apply to them. After several years of banging on about how important it is to recycle most things, I have just about managed to get them to wash out empty baked bean cans and put them on the kitchen window sill. The journey from the window sill to the appropriate blue container, which stores the tins, is approximately ten feet. I know this is a long, arduous journey and can take at least thirty seconds, but my kids just can't get their heads round it. It is after all, their world that we are trying to save. But unfortunately many of the youth today aren't concerned about such trivia.

Uncle Tony was in charge of igniting the fire. This he did by soaking the exposed timbers and debris on and around the fire with gallons of petrol. He always did this when no one was looking. He would then stick a lone sky rocket inside an empty milk bottle, roughly gauge its trajectory, light the missile, stand back, and watch the panic erupt. What Uncle T never did was bother to notify any of the spectators, some of whom were still placing wood on the fire. In the ensuing mayhem, kids would be blown off their feet and sport some wonderfully novel haircuts, full body waxing and facial hair removal. I think Uncle Tony perhaps contributed to the making of *Batman* when one year he unexpectedly created the face of the Joker on my Great-Grandmother.

During the morning of the following day, all the kids would meet up at the fire site and sift through the ashes looking for hidden treasures, all of which would be burnt and charred beyond recognition. This exercise involved prodding and poking with long sticks, and was somewhat of an art form. I don't know what it is about fire and sticks that so mesmerises and fascinates boys, but raking over embers and sifting through cinders provided great enjoyment and wonderment to our gang. The fact that the fire itself was still smouldering and could reignite at any time didn't deter us in the slightest.

One of our mates named Bones had his shoes catch on fire on more than one occasion. I think this was mainly due to his hand-me-down shoes. Poor old Bones was only a slight lad and resembled a racing snake. He had small feet, but because his family were so poor he was given second-hand shoes from all and sundry. It didn't matter that the majority of the cast-offs were several sizes too big—his mother would just stuff the toe ends with old newspaper until the shoes didn't fall off her lad's feet. He walked like Claude Hopper, (a comic book clown in the circus) but was a lot less steady on his feet. Bones would fall over thin air and spent more time on his arse than his feet. When he was painstakingly carrying out his investigation of the smouldering grey ashes, he was so transfixed with the task in hand, he never once noticed the smoke belching from his oversized, rubber-soled beetle-crushers—probably because his feet occupied so little space within them. I couldn't comprehend his lack of feeling or loss of smell, as the thick, acrid smoke drifted upwards into his nostrils. But with the speed of one of Uncle Tony's rockets, we would all witness the nearest thing to spontaneous combustion as Bones caught fire. Webbo was always on hand though, and to the relief of Bones and the onlookers, would quickly whip out his willy and dowse the flames in milli-seconds.

Bonfire Night is now a tradition on the brink of extinction. Certain people set off fireworks these days in order to alert drug addicts that they are in their vicinity with their deadly merchandise. Others do it to cause pain and suffering to dog owners and parents with young children. And all these mindless acts are carried out months prior to the main event and at all hours of the day and night. Fireworks have become bigger, more powerful, easily accessible, cheaper, and a lot more dangerous. Having fires causes global warming and is frowned upon. But on a good note, petrol is a great deal more expensive. So the old impromptu explosions and cluster infernos created by uncle T have all but ceased in the UK—and now moved to Iraq.

Chapter 9

Snow Wonder

As Christmas approached, children's thoughts were somewhat distracted from their forthcoming presents from Santa Claus and onto something far more spectacular and exciting—the first snow of the season. When it snowed in my early childhood, boy did it snow! One night you would go to bed and the world around you looked drab and lifeless. Next morning, however, you'd wake to a thick blanket of snow, four feet deep, and covering everything in sight. Grandad loved it when it snowed because he said it was the only time our garden looked like everyone else's.

Kids would race downstairs, skip washing and breakfast, don their balaclavas and gloves, and scoot outside to play. The crispness of the air carried the sound of laughter for miles. Children would have "apple cheeks" and smile incessantly. (I know the term *apple cheeks* is a little American, but I always thought it profoundly descriptive.) Grandad, however, used different terminology for this expression—he would say that the kids had faces like "slapped arses," but Grandad had a fixation with the word *arse* and would bring it into conversation at every opportune—and inopportune moment. When he came down to breakfast, he would always enlighten us with his words of wisdom and vividly let us in on his previous night's reverie. One of his favourite dreams he would share with the family was the one about his arse being a lemon, and all the family were sucking it! Another one was when his arse became a circus, and we were all eager to climb in unseen.

Once the boys and girls had escaped their parents' clutches and moved out of earshot, all the lads would take off their headgear and reposition it so the front face holes of their balaclavas went over their heads, and the frilled neck collars, which resembled the gills of a Komodo dragon, were used to peer through. Balaclavas worn in this fashion enabled the boys to look like frogmen. (Why boys wanted to look like frogmen in the snow is still a mystery to this day.)

Once the kids altered their attire, two teams would form, and each team would claim a side of the street as their territory. Battle would commence when the opposite sides were ready, laden with as many snowballs as they could make in twenty seconds. The ferocity and accuracy of some of those snowballs whizzing through the air and connecting with their targets was a joyous sight for parents to behold. Seeing their loved ones blinded and disabled must have brought tears to their eyes. It certainly did with most of the assembled troops. The battles never lasted longer than five minutes, and the blood-stained snow resembled a screwball ice cream, complete with decorative marbling. After a quick wash down in the icy slush, the battle recommenced.

It lasted only several seconds before the immortal words of Grandad rang out, "Be careful or someone will lose an eye!"

No one ever did lose an eye, apart from Tubby Skingley, who lost his glass eye down a drain in the school yard whilst he was playing marbles. Tubby had sported a glass eye from the age of two due to an unfortunate accident caused by his father's index finger.

Grandad always knew best, so the war was deemed a tie. We all limped off to the square at the end of our street to make a snowman. Constructing a snowman took time and effort because our snowman had to be bigger than that of our real enemies, the rival gangs from Devonshire Road and Norfolk Place. To begin our quest to build a monumental Jack Frost (not to be confused with the detective played by David Jason), we would recruit all the children who were out playing at the time (even the girls) and start by making a simple snowball. This would then be placed on the ground and carefully but firmly rolled forwards, gathering momentum and more snow, which allowed it to grow bigger and bigger with every thrust. When it became too big and heavy for one child, several children would form a synchronised team and manhandle it to where the ice statue was to be built.

With the expertise of the Egyptian pyramid builders and the grace of elephants, slowly but surely a white figure would begin to appear from the mass of snow. When Ginner decided it was to his specific measurements, work would halt, and the fine art of crafting and sculpting the face and body shape began. This was always carried out by Webbo because he was the tallest. Carrying out the refinements always took time, but all the assembled audience of children stood there in complete silence, eyes wide open with anticipation, marvelling at the wonderment of the creation of our ice man. Not one person uttered a word whilst Webbo weaved his magic, carving out the eyes and mouth and adorning it with Grandad's old hat and pipe. Finally, twigs were inserted in each side to look like arms, and small fragments of coal were plopped into the eye sockets.

It was at this precise moment, just when the eyes were fixed, that an eerie and uncertain feeling of terror swept over the congregation of boys and girls. I can only relate it to something biblical—or even magical. At any moment, this creation would come to life and begin to move. Staring, speechless and transfixed, the silence was shattered when the snowman's head fell clean off, directly at our feet, with its eyes staring menacingly skywards yet still trained on all of us. It was at this stage of the proceedings that at least six kids pissed their pants, one fainted, and my brother, Craig, filled his undercrackers with shit. Screams rang out, and all the kids legged it homewards, sprinting like leopards that'd had their knackers caught in a rat trap, not daring to glance back at the headless ice man.

A less frightening activity with regards to snow was one where all the local lads would get together and form a line several yards apart—well, at least out of view of parents and girls. On the count of three, each boy would release his tadger and proceed to pee in the snow. The idea was to either write your name with the flowing urine, or in Bones's case, see how far you could project the yellow spurt into the atmosphere. Bones was a legend among his peers at this trick and, such was his accuracy and skill, could take a gnat's eye out at twelve feet. God only knows how he managed such a feat of power and volume from his needle knob, but he did—and it impressed all of the gang every time we witnessed the genius of his wand! Writing our names proved less entertaining and somewhat unfair. If your name was Dan, you were in with a chance of winning. If, however, you were called Archibald, you obviously had a lesser chance of snatching first prize. I still find myself playing this game on the odd occasion, usually in the freezer section of our local supermarket!

It's a pity that it doesn't snow like it used to in years gone by. I truly feel that today's youngsters are missing out on such a good time. Sledging, making ice slides, and doing the "diddy-men", snow-balling, building snowmen, missing school because the cold snap had broken the central heating, writing your name with your own wee—and all this cost nothing. Kids aren't allowed to play in the real sense of the word anymore. This kind of play helped to build lasting friendships and taught us all one important lesson in life—don't eat yellow snow—not ever!

Chapter 10

A Dog Called Kesh

One spring day, I happened to come across what I thought was a dead fox, lying in the side of a hedge-row opposite my Uncle Tony's allotment. On closer inspection, I realised the bundle of matted ginger fur, lying motionless and splattered with dried blood, was in fact a dog. As I neared the creature, I discovered that it was still alive. To my delight, the dog lifted his head with all the strength it could muster and smiled at me. When I say smiled, that is exactly what the hound appeared to do. It didn't bare its teeth in a snarl-like way or growl at me—it simply smiled. I knelt down beside the dog and cradled its head in my arms. It looked up into my eyes and slowly rubbed its head in my hands. I then found the bloody thing was well and truly flea-ridden, but I didn't let it spoil our first acquaintance. It also became clear to me, looking at the blood stains in the lane, that it must have been knocked over by a car or tractor. The lane was now empty of traffic and people, and the only two visible things were me and the dog. He seemed in a bad way, but I felt an immediate affinity towards him. (I knew he was a male dog because he had a gigantic pair of "goolies" on show, which seemed blood-free and full of dog-sperm.) This dog and I bonded there and then—it was as simple as that.

After several minutes of stroking the mutt's head and talking to it in a silly baby-like way, reassuring him he would be fine, I decided to try and move him. This I did by placing my anorak on the ground beside him, and gently but firmly sliding him along onto the coat in small, spasmodic movements. The dog proved to be a star and tried to aid me whilst he struggled to get himself onto the coat. He managed to pull himself forward with his front legs, just far enough to reach the hood of my coat, and then he collapsed. I quickly put my hands under his rear end and carefully slid him fully onto the garment. It was then I realised that somewhere along the line he'd had a shit, which I only found out about when I picked him up. Within fifteen minutes of meeting my new canine friend, I was covered both in fleas and dog shit.

Having successfully manoeuvred the pooch onto my coat, I enterprisingly tied the arms of the anorak together to form a carrying handle and placed it over my head so it rested on my neck like a sling. The dog was now suspended in front of me, leaning against my chest. My first point of call would be Uncle Tony's. He would advise me on what to do in the circumstances. When I arrived at his house, Uncle T was inspecting his beloved cabbages. Tony took one look at the dog and told me to take it to the nearby pond, fill up the coat with bricks whilst the dog was still in it, and throw it into the water. The pond he referred to was affectionately known in Maltby as the *Dog Broth*. It was a dreadful stretch of dank, putrid water where people killed their unwanted pets. Obviously, seeking Uncle Tony's advice proved fruitless. I should have remembered his response to the constant noise of a neighbour's dog who barked for three days without a break—Uncle Tony shot it!

I made my way home, shattered with the strain from the weight of the injured hound, and finally reached my destination. My Mum came out to greet me. Without any warning, I received a clip around the lug-hole for being late and for being dirty—but when she realised I was transporting a dog that was hurt, her mood changed. Mum immediately took complete control of the situation. She never once complained about taking this stray dog into our humble abode and making it a member of the family. Mother did suggest, however, that I move out to make room for the dog.

We named the dog "Kesh" for no apparent reason, but he seemed to like it and responded to it straight away. Craig and I loved Kesh from day one, and he became as close to us as anyone or any thing. The great thing about dogs is their undying love and loyalty for their owners. It doesn't matter what kind of shitty day you've had and how crappy you feel, a dog always greets you with such affection and happiness—as if you've been away for years. It doesn't care what you look like, smell like, dress like—it just loves you for being you. (It's a pity human beings can't feel like this with each other.) Kesh would greet us with his full complement of teeth showing, as if he was smiling at us. When Mum took him to the vet's surgery later that day, we found out he had been run over by a car and had lost three of his toes on his left back leg. His remaining toe had been elongated, and from it, a one inch flat claw projected. What impressed me most about the hound was that despite the fact that he was nearing death's door when I found him, he'd still managed to raise a smile.

All the gang took to Kesh and loved him. We suddenly had a new mate who gave us the excuse of roaming farther from our regular haunts and into the woods that backed onto the fields we played in. Mum told us that Kesh required exercising to help build up his strength, especially in his hind quarters. We needed no other reason to adhere to her wishes and make for the hills with our canine companion.

On one such expedition, out of the blue, Kesh pricked up his ears and stopped stone dead. He raised his snout into the evening air and breathed in slowly and deeply, checking out the different odours wafting over him. In the blink of an eye, he set off running like a bullet, straight into a copse of trees in front of us. Prior to this, Kesh had always walked to heel so we had no reason to put him on a leash. What had he smelt? Where had he gone? We started to panic, and it crossed my mind that perhaps we'd lost him for good. He had never left my side for nearly three months now and, all of a sudden, he was gone—nowhere to be seen. We searched the woods for two hours, but to no avail. I started to feel sick inside and struggled to contain my emotions. Several members of the gang also felt the way I did, and my brother Craig, began to cry.

Just as I was reaching breaking point, I heard a man's voice calling out in the distance some fifty yards away. I couldn't make out exactly what he was shouting, but the words "bollocks" and "fanny" were quite distinct. As I drew nearer to the commotion, I could vaguely make out the shape of two people who seemed to be entwined together on the ground. I wiped my tear-stained eyes, and to my shock and horror, saw a naked man lying on top of a naked woman. Both looked like they were frozen in fear, quite still and not daring to move. The reason for their terror was Kesh, who stood directly behind the man. I then made my presence known to the couple, and in doing so, positioned myself in a better vantage point to assess the situation. The scene I witnessed on that day has scarred my memory for all eternity. I was old enough to understand that they were engaging in the art of making babies—they were both naked, and he was on top of her. The thing that puzzled me was

71

the sight of my dog, licking the "arse conkers" out of the man's anus. (*What was that all about?*) When I instructed the dog to cease its activity, it promptly stopped for breath and then proceeded to lick the guy's knackers.

The irate man then screamed at me, "Get your flea-ridden tripe hound off me, or I'll kill the pair of you!" He then proceeded to shout more unpleasant obscenities at both me and the mutt, but no matter what I said to Kesh, it made no difference. He was obviously enjoying the cheese and onion flavours of the man's genitals.

At this stage, the woman also started to swear at me, saying, "What kind of pervert teaches his dog to lick men's bollocks?"

She added that she was going to string me and the dog up naked over a telegraph wire and shoot at our testes with an air rifle. I didn't like the sound of that so I decided to make a hasty retreat. If Kesh valued his bollocks, he had better follow me—and quickly. As I began to turn away from the performance, Kesh abruptly halted his deep cleaning and turned to face me. As the man started to stand up, I decided it was time to make myself scarce and set off homeward bound, not daring to look back. Fortunately, the dog followed me.

The last parting words I heard were the man's, yelling at his girlfriend, "I wouldn't mind, but I was just on the "vinegar stroke" when that bastard dog joined in."

Not only did he find it unnerving having a strange dog entering his fun and frolics, but apparently, he was pissed off with the dog's timing. I wanted to tell him there and then that our dog's timing was spot on and he was barking up the wrong tree, but considering the circumstances, I thought the better of it.

Another eventful day out with my dog occurred when Grandad decided that due to the hound being ill (he was a little loose at the backend), he would come out for a walk and check up on the consistency of the dog's business, so to speak. Kesh could crap for England and no sooner had we reached the playing fields, than he was squatting like a good'un and emptying his bowels. It was dusk at the time so the light was fading, making it hard to see clearly. Grandad requested that I lean over where the dog had dumped and inspect it for worms and things. Knowing what Grandad was like for playing practical jokes, I informed him I was suffering from a bad back and suggested he do it. Grandad was surprisingly sympathetic to my ailment and duly bent down to examine the dog's "do-do".

Kesh had now finished his movement, and just when Grandad was peering into the shit, about twelve inches away, Kesh did what dogs do after a crap and kicked up his rear feet several times. I think this is a dog's version of wiping its arse. Now Kesh inadvertently moved forward, slightly in front of his mess, and instead of kicking up fresh air and a bit of grass, managed to deftly propel dog diarrhoea right across Grandad's face. He jumped up with a howl and, mouth agog, threw up all over the dog. What a photograph this would have made: Grandad covered in freckles, and Kesh looking like a pepperoni pizza!

Having a dog like Kesh certainly enriched our lives. He was a real character and a dog lothario. He loved bitches with a passion, and they loved him. He would regularly go missing for days at a time, in search of his favourite pastime. You could always tell when he was getting ready for his next assignment. He would sit at the front door panting and exhibiting his dog member for the entire world to see. My Mum would refer to his huge appendage as his *half a yard of salmon* or his *lipstick*. Kesh was not a proud dog, or indeed, an obedient one. When he got the scent of another bitch in heat, he could smell it for miles, just as a shark can detect minute quantities of blood in vast amounts of water. It was just a case of someone failing to shut the door properly, and he was off.

One morning as Craig and I were heading off to school, a policeman arrived at our house to inform us that our dog had been run over. This was obviously not the first time. He told us of the dog's location and added he was still alive, but in a weak state. We zoomed off like the wind to attend to our beloved hound. Fearing the worst, we raced through the streets. As we turned onto Salisbury Road, we spotted him lying completely motionless beside a gate.

When we neared him and called his name, he raised his head and smiled in a way only he could. I bent over him and gently stroked his head, looking for visible signs of damage through his fur. To my relief, I couldn't find any, and he looked and felt fine to me. The one thing I did notice was a pungent aroma coming off his body that made my eyes smart. I had smelt this dog fragrance on Kesh before and associated it with his sexual conquests. When Mum arrived at the scene, she realised immediately that the dog hadn't been knocked over by a vehicle at all. He had been out on the town, so to speak, with one of his floozies and, by the looks of things, had been having his wicked way with her all night. The only reason he was lying down and not moving was the fact that he was completely exhausted from his night's activities. Our dog was the canine equivalent of Casanova, and even Casanova needed a rest once in a while. The dog was so tired Mum had to carry him all the way home like a wounded, heroic soldier. The look of triumph and satisfaction on that dog's face will live with me forever—one of total accomplishment.

Having a randy dog living with you is one thing, but a dog that farted for Europe and could scrape his arse along the floor for distances up to twelve feet was quite another. His farting prowess was legendary in our house, but I honestly think when I look back, Grandad should have taken some of the credit for the dog's anal expulsions. He always blamed Kesh for the acrid smell, which you could taste in the atmosphere when you were around the pair of them. When we shouted at Kesh for his smelly misdemeanours, he would just look into our eyes and smile. At this sight, we would instantly forgive him.

Whilst I'm writing this and recalling the memories, I can see in my mind's eye Grandad, standing over the dog, laughing at him and us and telling us one of his favourite jokes about a man who came home from the pub drunk with a Great Dane. The next morning, his wife went downstairs naked to collect the post. When she bent over to pick up the letters from the floor, the dog mounted her from the rear. Later that day, she took the dog to the vet. Whilst she was in the waiting room, she told the vet's assistant what had happened that morning with her and the dog. The horrified assistant asked her if she had brought the dog to the vet to have it put down.

The woman replied, "Oh no! I'm going to get the vet to cut his nails!"

If Grandad told us that joke once, he told it us a hundred times. The thing is, though, he always found it funny, as if he'd told it for the very first time.

Chapter 11

School Days at St Mary's

Growing up is never easy or straightforward. Added to this, the prospect of having to go to school was something we dreaded. Attending a Catholic school was a punishment in itself. The teachers were strict, and discipline was the order of the day.

When I chat to people about their childhood memories of school, their recollections are always happy ones that bring smiles to their faces. My memories are somewhat different. When I was five years old, I vividly remember a boy being caught acting daft and naughty in a lesson. Nowadays, people would say that he was just expressing himself. He was dragged to the front of the class, had his shorts along with his underwear pulled down to his ankles, bent over the teacher's knee, and spanked on the bare arse six times. Today's establishments of ill repute ask people to pay for this form of punishment, but this was a bloody classroom. And *I* couldn't sit down for a week afterwards! Whilst the teacher in question was doling out her chastisement, I was worrying about the other spanking I was going to get back home when Mum found out that I'd been messing about in class.

In days gone by, corporal punishment was rife. Teachers would hit kids with slippers, canes, rulers, board rubbers, hands, and occasionally, swords. (Ok, I made the last item up for dramatic effect.) Having been on the receiving end of several good hidings or beatings, I can honestly say, hand on heart, it never affected my growing up in any way, apart from my homicidal psychotic tendencies and my stutter—oh, and the recurring nightmares and flashbacks, and my dependency on hard drugs. In hindsight, I would have been better off with the Yanks when they went into Vietnam. The flashbacks would have subsided by now.

In the village where I spent my early years, most of the people I knew or associated with were poor. No one pretended to be anything different, other than a pauper or street urchin. Kids didn't wear designer clothes. Some kids didn't have clothes. Maltby was, and still is, a hard place in which to reside. It has grown over the years, but is fiercely proud of its association with the mining industry. Both my Grandads worked down the pit all their lives, and in the end, diseases and illness relating to pits attributed to both their untimely deaths. If you asked people back then why they worked in the colliery, they would either answer, "Because I have to," or "So my kids don't have to."

Coming home from their shifts with coal dust in their eyes was the nearest thing a miner got to being in touch with his feminine side. When we were woken up as children, we used to suffer from a sticky secretion in the corners of our eyes. If you were from a posher or more affluent part of the north, this was sometimes referred to as "sleep dust" or "fairy powder". In Maltby, we just called it "gowl"! There was nothing fairy or powder about the gunk in our eyes, just good old, dried-up gowl.

Another childhood problem we had back then was head lice. Everyone suffered from this at school at least two or three times a year. Each term, the "nit nurse" would visit our school and scour the heads of children, searching for head lice. She would bend us over, very roughly I might add, and rake a fine comb through our greasy locks with the grace of a ham-fisted, punch-drunk boxer until she found some of the itchy critters, or until our heads bled!

Once again, the kids in Maltby didn't refer to head lice as nits. No—we referred to them as "dicks", which seemed far more appropriate—especially when shouting across the street to your mate, "Hey dick-head," as opposed to, "Hey nithead." Dickhead had more balls and sounded a lot harder. It gave the child more credibility and standing in society in general.

One of my old mates at school was a guy known as "Picker Licker". He whiled away the hours during lessons daydreaming, with his index finger buried up to his third knuckle in his nose. It never ceased to amaze me how far he could insert his digit up his nasal passage and for how long. He seemed to be in a world of his own, slowly and methodically mining his two lineal caves for "bogeys" or "crows," as we used to call them. It didn't matter a jot to him when the teacher told him that if he carried on picking his nose, his head would cave in.

His classmates would walk past him and shout, "Pick us a winner, mate."

But Picker Licker carried on his relentless pursuit of nasal exploration—to find and eat the world's biggest, juiciest bogey. It was a passion for him, and he seemed oblivious to the rest of us. Picker would also store some of his treasures underneath his desk for mid-afternoon snacks.

One day, a supply teacher came into our class-room and made all the children change places with each other to stop them from talking during lesson time. Poor Jane Junior had the unfortunate luck of being seated in Picker's chair. All went well for the first ten minutes, until Jane inadvertently put her hands underneath the desk and got covered in Pickers hidden cache of bogeys, some of which were still moist. On closer examination of her hands, she realised what the offending items were and went totally berserk. The paddy she threw that day still haunts me, and I attribute this incident to the start of my obsessive-compulsive disorder, which makes me constantly pick my snout, then wash my hands.

During lesson times, I used to like to drift off and think of birds and wildlife which were, and still are, my passion in life. I believe all children should be encouraged to daydream and let their minds wander for at least thirty minutes a day to allow space for their minds to develop and let creativity flow. I get really pissed off when I see the pressure kids are put under today in order that they pass exams—just to make headmasters and teachers look good, and in turn, make the arseholes who run the country look even better. Passing exams involves having good short-term memory retention. Knowledge without understanding is worthless. Children learn at different speeds, and some kids need motivating and coaching to enable them to realise their true potential. But the biggest thing children need is time.

We live in a fast world with ever changing technology, and people are encouraged to strive for bigger and better things. Nowadays, people want to be famous for just being famous. They crave wealth and power and all the trappings that go with it. If this is the true way forward, why are so many people in society depressed and unhappy? Why is violence so prolific and crime on the increase? Well, if you asked me these questions I wouldn't have a bleeding clue, because I'm too busy counting my ill-gotten gains on my luxury yacht in Puerto Banus, Marbella, from the numerous East European prostitutes I employ.

On one of my "castles in the air" trips into my subconscious, I found myself imagining life as a bird, wind beneath my wings, circling the thermals and soaring effortlessly though the atmosphere. I had left the classroom environment and began to concentrate my thoughts on time and space. During my inner journey, the teacher noticed my glazed expression, as had the rest of my classmates. Silence descended on the room, and all eyes fell on me. Unbeknownst to me, she had asked me a question on church congregations. (I couldn't answer the bloody question now, never mind then.) She asked me several times, and finally, after telling me the answer was "not out of the window," she clapped her hands loudly in front of my face.

Startled and somewhat bewildered, I stood bolt upright and said, "Shit on the bastards below."

The entire class burst into laughter, and the look of horror on her face said to me that I was in big trouble, as this was obviously not the answer she had in mind. In my dream-like state, I'd been recalling a football song to myself which goes like this:

If I had the wings of a sparrow,
The dirty great arse of a crow,
I'd fly over the Crag School tomorrow,
And shit on the bastards below!

Sung to the tune of 'My Bonny Lies over the Ocean'

When she woke me from my dream-like state, I was on the last part of the song, and zombie-like, had just stood up and recited it like urban poetry. She sent me straight to the headmaster whose answer to the world's problems was "six of the best," which was six whacks across my arse with a wooden cane. After helping me off the office floor and injecting morphine into my bloodstream for pain relief, the headmaster said that he wasn't offended by the word "bastard," but by the reference to the Crag School. He said I should have called it the Manor School.

"But I was daydreaming, sir, and I only recited the last line of the song that I'd been taught by you on the school trip last year," I said.

"But that was then, and this is now, boy! Have you forgotten that the Manor School beat us last week at rounders?"

Enough said!

Both the Crag School and Manor School were Protestant institutions and not Catholic like ours. "Prody dogs" were always at war with us and referred to us as "Catalogues". After school was over, you were cast out through the gates onto the streets, and it was boys and girls for themselves. Invariably, we were greeted by rival factions of gangs from other schools, baying for our blood with sticks and stones. We were taught the old saying: "Sticks and stones may break my bones, but names will never hurt me." Well, I for one would have loved it if our enemies would just stick to name-calling. Sticks and bloody stones *do* break bones. I had my finger broken with a stick and nearly lost the sight in my eye with a stone.

It didn't matter if the mums and dads were there to meet their offspring after a day's tutoring. The hoards of infantile yobs, both boys and girls, would still be waiting, making the kids from our school run the "gauntlet of fear," which stretched for fifty yards. The physical and verbal abuse hurled upon us made us even kinder people—*kinda shit scared*! Watching the masses of children squeeze through the tiny school gate was like observing sand through an egg-timer, but a hundred times quicker. Smaller tots would be trampled upon by their elders, and looking back on this debacle, parents should have known better and somehow protected their kids. It was like a scene from a wildlife documentary, where all the wildebeest met up at a small, crocodile-infested crossing point at the mouth of a river—only one way across—and the wildebeest just kept coming in their droves, more and more, pushing those at the front farther forward into the jaws of their enemies.

On one particular day, terrified youngsters clung to their siblings for help and protection. Parents screamed in sheer desperation at the whole situation erupting in front of their very eyes. When the strain and suffering began to take its toll, and just before someone was about to lose an eye, the headmaster from our school appeared, like Alexander the Great, and summoned everyone to stop. At this mighty command from a fearless leader, the assembled crowd looked up in total awe and admiration and then completely ignored him. From behind enemy lines, a large rock was propelled at great speed and accuracy, which hit the headmaster plumb square between the eyes, instantly breaking his nose and knocking him out cold. None of the rioters gave a flying shit what a Catalogue headmaster said to them.

It would have been wonderful if the head teacher had been a bit more attuned to his faith and said, "Let he who has not sinned cast the first stone." But alas, this was not the case.

As I stared into the mob, I just glimpsed our local priest at the rear of the crowd. Camouflaged as a Protestant, he was running off into the nearby labyrinth of terraced houses, stones falling from his rucksack as he fled.

When the battle had finished, all the children from their respective gangs left peacefully so they wouldn't be late for their supper. The Catholic kids just brushed themselves down and went home in an orderly fashion, looking forward to the repeat performance the following day.

Race discrimination was very much evident in my early years, but back then, no one was really in a position to help so we just accepted it. Being from Irish Catholic stock on my grandma's side, and with some Geordie and Jewish bloodline on my grandfather's, I was every racist's dream catch. The irony of it all was that most of my closest and best mates were good old 'C of E' (Church of England). We fought after school because that's what we thought we had to do—the only difference being that after the mass brawls we were all friends again, and no one carried any bad blood until we met up after school again the following day. There would be the odd occasion when I would secretly piss through Ginner's letter box in his front door and set fire to Webbo's fence—but that was all down to tomfoolery on my part, and no malice was ever intended.

Coming home from school on one occasion, Craig and I were stopped by two larger lads at the Queens Corner, which was and still is, pretty much the centre of Maltby. It was approximately 4:15 in the afternoon, and the streets were packed with shoppers and mums and dads. The boys looked rather menacing and were up for a rout. The uglier of the two asked Craig if he was a Prodidog or a Catalogue. Craig looked at me shit-scared and replied to the boy that he was neither. This somehow took the wind out of the lad's sails.

"Well, what are you then, if you're not a Prodidog or a Catalogue?" the lad went on to say in rather angry tones.

"I'm a 'Prologue'," Craig replied.

The two boys stared intently at each other and then stared at Craig and me. Looking somewhat bemused and dumbfounded with the answer they received, they said that was okay and bid us a good evening. Off we trotted home, feeling pretty chuffed with Craig's retort. Craig was always a "foreword" sort of guy!

The only other scary moment we encountered like this one was on a dark September evening, again on our way home from school, and again at the same junction in Maltby. When this incident occurred, the teenager in question who stopped us was in a different league to our normal foes. He stood a good six feet tall and was covered in tattoos from head to toe. His two front teeth were missing, and he only had half a nose. He walked with a limp and had no ears. (I think you've got the picture.) The thing that completely threw me, though, was that he answered to the name Ginger, which sounded similar to my mate's name, and I wondered if they were related. It was then that I happened to notice one of his tattoos with the words *Hell's Angles* written on it, as opposed to *Hell's Angels*. Yes, *Hell's Angle*s. Having noticed the misspelling of the word *angels*, I suddenly felt this surge of laughter begin to make its way from my belly to my mouth. Thinking quickly on my feet, whilst trying to suppress my guffawing, I realised to my peril that I was on the verge of instant death. To make matters worse, I noticed Craig staring at the dude with the terrified expression of a rabbit staring into the headlights of a car. On seeing Craig's fixation, the guy asked him what he was looking at. To give my brother his due, he has always had a razor-sharp wit and is quick off the draw.

Craig took a ponderous look at the guy again and exhibited great concern for him, saying, "You've got lovely eyes, mate. You should look after those eyes. They could make you a fortune."

"What do you mean I've got lovely eyes and should look after them?" the youth replied, looking slightly puzzled at Craig's retort.

"Well, mate, having noticed that the sides of your head are minus ear holes and taking into account you can still hear me, you'll never be able to wear glasses, will you?" was Craig's swift reply.

At this, we set off home like the wind, crying with laughter all the way. The fact that we were shitting our pots full as we sped along made the incident even funnier.

Chapter 12

Bird Nesting in King's Wood

My fascination with ornithology, or the study of birds, started in my very early childhood years. Like most people, the interest and pleasure stem from the ability to recognise a bird and name it. I love the Latin names for a bird, like the common blackbird whose Latin name is *Turdus merula*, or the humble wren whose Latin name is *Troglodytes troglodytes*. Their Latin names seem to sing and float off the tongue. I was also captivated and bewitched by their plumage and their songs. During the early 60s, it was still commonplace for boys to go hunting for birds' eggs in the spring and early summer months and most lads had an egg collection under their beds or in their drawers upstairs at home. The Protection of Birds Act 1967, which came into force on the 14th January 1968, made stealing certain birds' eggs a criminal offence—so of course it became even more popular around that time, and therefore, some bird species teetered on the brink of extinction.

When I was growing up, the summers seemed longer and warmer than they are now, with a lot less rain. When people over the age of sixty recall the "long, hot summers of childhood," they are not being misguided by nostalgia because they were born in a period of relative warmth, and their recollections are real and true.

The two main forces that governed the peaks and troughs of British bird life are climate and man's manipulation of his surroundings and environment. Farmers were given grants for ripping out hedgerows, which in turn, decimated wildlife in general. Decades on, the same farmers are given subsidies to replant hedgerows, which encourage wildlife to return. In the name of progress, mankind marches on, relentlessly taking control of great swathes of land and forests in order to change the environment to suit his needs. He builds dams and diverts rivers for his own require-ments, and not a thought is given to the millions of insects and animals who have inhabited these same pastures and woodlands for centuries. Man should embrace nature and learn to respect it.

Education is the answer, and governments should be pumping money into making mankind aware of its actions before its too late. We should redress the balance between man and nature and learn from it. All the cures for the world's diseases are here on earth in some form or another—we just need to find them. You cannot do this, however, if we are ripping up vast acres of the rainforests each day and pumping billions of tonnes of carbon dioxide into the atmos-phere, slowly choking the earth to death. Whilst I am writing this, I realise my conscience has been pricked and I ought to sell the huge amount of shares I have invested in China, America, and India. The returns are bloody marvellous at the moment. I should also trade in that new Hummer automobile I only use for the school runs. (We all must do our bit for the envi-ronment, and think green.)

On the subject of birds in general, it gladdens my heart to witness the rise in population of birds of prey. During the 60s and 70s, thousands of beautiful raptors were wiped out by chemical poisons. Once again, ignorance played a huge part in their downfall. Farmers and hunters were fed propaganda from the "powers that be," and misinformed about the real issues at large. If you have ever seen a sparrow hawk, or *Accipiter nisus*, swoop down with lightning speed and accuracy and take its prey with the ferocity and agility of a martial arts expert, you have been truly blessed. These hawks, like all birds of prey, are meat eaters, hunt for their food, have hooked beaks and kill with their feet. Raptors, from the Latin *Raptare*, which translates to "seize or to grasp," grip their quarry with their lethal talons and are skilful predators.

I was privileged once to see a sparrow hawk attack and kill a blue tit. Early one July morning, I was sitting silently in the King's Wood when along the ground at a height of maybe two feet, I saw this majestic creature flying like a stealth bomber, radar locked on its prey and silent as the night. The thing that struck me the most was the speed and impact of the kill. It was awesome. The sheer elegance and aerial manoeuvring of the hawk was astounding. Just when I thought it couldn't get any better, I managed to catch a glimpse of the bird's eyes. The eyes of a ruthless assassin engaged on the one thing it does best—kill.

Suddenly, I was startled by the sound of a gunshot. The *crack* of the barrel and the *thud* of the strike rattled my bones, and I threw myself flat to the ground. My heart was racing, and cold perspiration trickled down the back of my neck. I laid there motionless, petrified from the loud *bang,* which split the peace and tranquillity of the soft morning air. Not daring to move, I heard the sound of crushing twigs, getting ever nearer with each step. In situations like these, I just tend to freeze.

Lying there motionless, not daring to breathe or move for fear of being spotted, the sound of gun boots drew nearer. I could sense the presence of a person standing over me through my tightly closed eyes.

"What the bloody hell are you doing here, Alf?" a man's voice said, laughing while he spoke.

I recognised those dulcet tones. With a sigh of relief, coupled with the smell of relief in my trousers, I hauled myself up onto my feet. Uncle Tony stood there, larger than life, with a cocked shotgun in his hand.

"Did you see me blast that pigeon out of the hawthorn tree, boy?" Uncle Tony said.

"That wasn't a pigeon. It was a sparrow hawk, and it had just killed its breakfast," I replied.

"Well, I've just killed mine. Hey, look at this, Alf. Can you believe it? I've killed two birds with one bullet. I'm the dog's bollocks with a gun, son."

I remember thinking to myself, *What a heartless bastard, but what an amazing shot.*

I was too upset to carry on this conversation. I nodded to him in a disapproving sort of way and made myself scarce. I was truly blessed that day, and the sight of that king amongst birds will live with me forever. I often wonder whether or not Uncle Tony ate the birds. Alas, he's not here any longer for me to ask.

Later on in my youth, a film was made called 'Kes,' chronicling the experiences of a young northern boy who finds a kestrel and trains it. Their relationship becomes symbolic of the harsh realities of trying to escape the poverty and emptiness of the industrial North. I loved this film with a passion and still do. It is a compassionate film that truly reflects how life really was back then. The acting is first class, and the locations still manage to transport me back in time to my childhood years. If you haven't seen this film, I recommend you go and buy it or rent it. It's fantastic!

When I went out looking for birds' nests, the sole reasoning behind it was so that I could pilfer the eggs I didn't already have in my collection. On my expeditions, I always went alone. This was mainly due to the fact that when I went nesting with gang members, they always made too much noise and scared the birds from their nesting sites well before I could locate their exact positions. Now when I go out walking in the woods, I always tend to be by myself to minimise sound and observe as much of the natural wildlife as I can, undisturbed. Looking back on my "egging" adventures, I realise now that stealing eggs was, and is, wrong. We did, however, adhere to a code of ethics when we were bird nesting:

1) Never take an egg which is warm. Not ever!
2) Never take more than one egg—unless you find a duck's nest.
3) Never take an egg if there is only one in the nest.
4) Always put eggs in your mouth when descending trees.
5) Always take a spoon with you in case of a blue tit's nest.
6) Never rag a bird's nest and destroy it.
7) Never take a girl nesting.
8) Never take Uncle Tony.

One May morning, I again found myself in King's Wood, which was situated on the outskirts of Maltby. The trees had been planted years ago and brimming with rare birds and wildlife. This wood was patrolled by a gamekeeper who was referred to as "One Eye and a Ball of Chalk," for reasons I know not. He was a stocky man with a filthy temper, and if he ever caught you trespassing or poaching, he would thrash you with a thumb stick, which he always held in his right hand.

Being alone and in touch with nature at grass roots level, I never got caught. I just seemed to blend in with my surroundings. This was indeed a good attribute to have when twitching, or bird-watching. It allowed you to observe so much more of what was going on around you. I could sit for hours, perched up a large sycamore tree, watching life itself unfold before my very eyes. I once observed one of my uncles playing naked "wheelbarrows" with a woman whilst I sat aloft a tree. But the majority of time I sat amongst the branches at the canopy level of the forest scanning the terrain for birds. King's Wood was teeming with the buggers—from common buzzards to nightingales.

It's funny to look back at this time of my life and recall how I could identify nearly every sedentary and migratory bird in the British Isles—their English names, Latin names, and even their countryside names, specific to where I lived. Colloquial names for birds interested me even more than their Latin names. A yellowhammer was locally called a *Scribble Lark* due to the identification marks on its eggs. A whitethroat was a N*ettle Peggy* because it that in made its nests in clumps of nettles. A *Jenny Wren* was a titmouse, etc.

I knew all this at such an early age, but because I didn't understand algebra in my maths lesson, I was classed as thick! I didn't understand algebra then and am proud to say that I don't comprehend it now.

91

I've never needed it in forty-odd years so I think I can honestly say it was a complete waste of my fucking time trying to learn it in the first place. Teachers just don't get it; maths is boring. They should be re-educated and made to teach maths differently so all the kids (not just the swots in the class and those with all their digits intact) understand it.

Teaching should be fun, and it should be mandatory that teachers are funny. To be able to relate to kids, you have to think like kids. It's that simple. Make the lessons humorous and involve the children in the actual lesson itself. Let boys and girls sing and be happy. Let them see that making mistakes and being different are fine and acceptable qualities to have. The road to genius is littered with mistakes. It's not all about winning or who's got the best clothes or the richest parents.

My own children have to make do with only one personal assistant apiece, and I limit their expense account to a mere £5,000 a month. I want them to realise the value of money, and that having your own credit card at the age of seven is okay so long as you pay off the minimum balance of accrued interest each month.

Perched in my hideout, high above the woodland floor, I noticed old "One Eye and a Ball of Chalk" poking in the undergrowth with his long staff, hoping to flush out a pheasant or two. He stopped momentarily, right below the tree where I sat. Because I was so high up in the canopy blending in with the dense foliage of the tree, I knew he couldn't see me. His dog, which was with him at the time, was as old and as deaf as he was so I felt relatively safe in my little nest. It was then I noticed him having a piss up against the trunk of the tree. It was windy at the time, and the breeze was whizzing around him, blowing his urine everywhere. It was at this precise time I was overcome with a feeling of sheer madness and decided to release my penis from its captive underpants and piss into the sky, showering him down below with what he thought was late morning dew. When I noticed him opening his mouth and savouring the yellow heavenly droplets of piss I decided to stop in midstream. I heard him mention something about "God's tears" and left it at that, thinking to myself, *Every dog has its day*.

Days spent in King's Wood were halcyon days for me. I felt that I was at one with nature, especially hidden up in the branches of old trees, far from the prying eyes of the world below. Here I would sit for hours on end, just observing nature and her secrets. Transporting myself back in time, hunched up a gnarled old oak tree, I recall an old friend of mine, Jane Moore. She was the only girl I knew back then to have a nickname relating to birds. We called her "moorhen," Latin name *Magnificus Tittius*.

I once found a five-egger Pied Wagtail's nest in a small cave adjacent the dyke when I was eight years old—and boy did this make me feel special. I also shagged a gorgeous blond girl who lied about her age when I was seventeen. This also made me feel very special (yes, you know who you are, Dirty Girty).

Chapter 13

Cousin Chesswood

When I was a kid, the thought of answering my teacher back or calling a policeman a "fuck wit" never crossed my mind. I just did what all kids did back then and stayed silent when getting told off. I always knew my place and knew that by trying to have my say in matters of who's right and who's wrong I would exacerbate the situation and get myself deeper into trouble. As a child, I was always wrong, according to my family, it was as simple as that. If I'd been arguing with Craig, my kid brother, and the disagreement turned into a fight, I knew that I would be severely punished whether I had started the altercation or not. In the event of a scrap with Craig, I would enter the affray armed with the knowledge of the impending beating from my Mum. And as the old adage goes, *You might as well get hung for a sheep as get hung for a lamb.*

So I would try to maim him or at least draw blood. I once knocked over his toy Air Fix soldiers that he'd been painstakingly setting up all morning for one of his mock battles. I protested my innocence to him and said I'd stumbled on the carpet. But he didn't buy my story, due to the fact that the soldiers had been positioned all across the living room floor, covering an area of at least twenty-five square yards, and numbered in the region of a thousand men. The inevitable fight erupted, and after a few punches to the head and several knees to the groin, I requested that we cease for a minute so I could put on my

94

Chelsea boots in order to kick him a damn sight harder in the bollocks. Being my younger brother and respecting my decision-making, he agreed. As I started to slip my boots on, Craig, noticing that I had both my hands full, promptly smashed me over the head with Grandad's tea mug. This wasn't like any ordinary mug; it could hold more hot liquid than a bath, and God was it heavy.

The next thing I remember was coming round in the hospital, draped in a blood-stained turban, with my mother saying to me, "Wait till you get home, lad. I'm going to give you such a hiding it will knock some sense into that thick head of yours." Mum always knew just what to say to make me feel better.

On my return home that evening, I had the unex-pected pleasure of meeting Chesswood, my cousin, for the first time. "Chessie," as we called him, was in his mid-twenties and a touch strange. He was of obese proportions and had the best pair of *moobs*, or man boobs, I had ever seen. He wore a blonde, curly wig with cascading ringlets, and positively dripped with fake jewellery. His face was caked in cheap makeup, and his permanent startled expression could only be replicated if you shoved a huge, fat stick right up your arsehole. He had sling-back high heel shoes— ladies' shoes, of course—and wore a peek-a-boo bra. Cousin Chessie was somewhat off the wall and never really fitted into society in general, but he didn't care. The only thing that Chessie had any interest in was Mr Blewit, who ran the local chip shop. Many a time, Chessie was given a battered onion ring by Mr Blewit, whether he asked for one or not.

During my initial encounter with cousin Chessie, I felt compelled to ask him why he was called Chesswood. I received no reply to my question so I trundled off into the next room and asked Grandad.

He explained that Chesswood had been arrested on his twenty-first birthday by the local police for driving through the centre of Maltby, bollock naked on a moped whilst declaring his undying love for Mr Blewit at the top of his drunken voice. When the police finally stopped him, they, along with the numerous shoppers who had dived for cover as Chessie careered through the plate glass window of the village supermarket, noticed that Chesswood had a penis the size of a button mushroom. (Chesswood is the brand name of popular tinned button mushrooms.) So from that day forth, he was known throughout Maltby as Chesswood. Following Grandad's eloquent story, I couldn't look at my cousin again without thinking of his nob.

Chessie was a fun guy (or *fungi* if you're still on the mushroom theme) and never complained about his moniker. You might like to know that throughout the British Isles, we have several species of mushroom with names like "cramp balls," "candle snuff," "stinkhorn," "giant puffballs" and, wait for it … "wood blewits." The latter are more commonly known as "blue stalks," and taste bloody marvellous. His world revolved around his beloved chip fryer, and that's all he cared about.

When I asked Grandad if it was normal behaviour for a man to dress up as a woman, he simply nodded. I decided to leave it at that. Chessie's dress sense left a lot to be desired. He spent hours perusing the charity shops in the nearby town looking for bargains. He always insisted on purchasing items of clothing that were far too small or tight for his enormous bulk so he resembled the Michelin Tyre Man. His elephantine naked body was said to be totally hairless, and it was once mentioned in conversation with my Uncle Jack that tattooed on the cheeks of his arse were the words *Please enter*. He apparently suffered from permanent "ring sting," and it was said that his backside resembled a blood orange. But he wasn't considered a homosexual by any of the family, as this was deemed to be sinful, especially in the eyes of our parish priest.

Chessie not only liked his food, he also loved his lager, which he referred to as "bitch piss". At a relative's christening, he apparently sank too much of the amber nectar before he entered the church and caused somewhat of a scene with the priest who was presiding over the baptism. He was convinced that the frocked curate fancied him so, in the middle of proceedings, he decided to spice things up by disrobing himself entirely of his ladies' apparel, apart from his Wellington boots. On his naked torso, he applied lipstick around his pierced nipples and began to make small talk with the priest. On seeing this obscene spectacle, the priest passed out and collapsed onto the floor. Fortunately Chessie was on hand to give him the "kiss of life".

The onlookers were mortified with my cousin for his outrageous behaviour, and he was swiftly bundled into the confessional booth, away from the prying eyes of the stunned children. Chessie was warned to stay there until he sobered up and got properly attired. Due to his state of complete insobriety, he fell asleep and missed the remainder of the christening, which was a blessing for the families involved. When he finally came to his senses, he realised that someone had entered the adjoining booth and had begun to make their confession to who they thought was the priest. The lady in question confessed to having oral sex with her boyfriend and asked my cousin what penance she would receive.

At this part of the proceedings, Chessie poked his head out of the booth and called out in hushed tones to a passing altar boy, "What does Father O'Fiddle normally give for oral sex?"

"A Mars bar and a can of coke," was the boy's reply.

Chesswood, in his infinite wisdom, decided this would be a good time to leave the church, but he did manage to get the lad's name and address on the way out. As he waddled through the churchyard, he caught sight of the priest and thought it only fair and proper to tender his apologies. He beckoned him over, but the churchman made a dash to the sanctuary of his presbytery. Chessie wasn't the fastest of movers so he declined the chase and made his way home.

Full of remorse the following day, Chessie decided to take the priest some flowers as a way of apologising. Now, my cousin was also renowned for being somewhat careful with his money. He didn't like the thought of parting with his immoral earnings as a part-time rent boy easily, so he reckoned on picking up some wildflowers on his way to church, probably from the churchyard itself. As luck would have it, he stumbled upon a clump of yellow blooms growing at the causeway edge and plucked them quickly, so as not to draw attention to himself. What he failed to realise is that a fat, transvestite hooker, wearing six-inch stiletto heels and wobbling like a jelly on a plate, can find no hiding place on the streets of Maltby.

A voice called out from across the road, "Why are you picking "*Piss-a-beds*," Chessie?"

Now, I feel that I should explain the fact that "*Piss-a-bed*" was a name given to the humble dandelion, which grows wild throughout the British Isles and classed as a weed. Folklore says that when picking the yellow flowers of this plant, you will be cursed during the night and piss the bed.

Out of embarrassment, Chessie dropped the flowers in fear that he could be wetting the sheets that night. After all, he was entertaining the altar boy he had met the previous day in the church, that evening, and didn't want to mess things up, literally.

"You don't want to be giving your special friend some weeds, do you?" asked the lad. "You should go down into the woods and pick him some '*Poke-Me-Gently*'," (Old name for Wood Anemone) he went on. Chessie liked this suggestion and asked the boy to join him for the afternoon. He promised the youngster that following the nature trip, he would take him to the cake shop and treat him to a *creamed horn*.

Now Chessie had a very close-knit group of friends back then. It was said by those who associated with my cousin that if you didn't know him, it would be very difficult to penetrate his inner circle! Chessie liked most men, but unfortunately, most men didn't like him. I put this down to the fact that he had breath that smelt like that of a bulldog, but I could have been mistaken. He would regularly frequent telephone kiosks and leave his contact details inside for people to get in touch with him. I felt sorry for him and deeply concerned that he needed to try to make new acquaintances in this way. I once managed to catch sight of one of his cards in the phone booth near our house. On it was a picture of a man's bare arse with the word *Somme* written across the buttocks. The caption below read: *This has seen more action, though!*

I didn't have a clue what this meant, but it somehow didn't feel right, so I decided to keep Chessie at a safe distance until I fully understood his intentions. My speculation about my cousin's bizarre behaviour resurfaced at the swimming baths. The first thing I noticed about him was his trunks—or lack of them. And at least a dozen small children were huddled together in the shallow end, all looking daunted and anaemic.

Chessie, however, was splashing about in the deep end of the pool like Moby Dick, shouting out to the kids, "Why don't you come up my end?"

I felt sorry for the little'uns because for them, it was either "muck or nettles," meaning they had to choose the lesser of two evils. It was either swimming in the icy, dank waters of the lido or facing the prospect of cousin Chesswood!

They were fortunately saved by the bell when Sid, the pool owner, appeared on the scene and cried out to Chessie, "Get out now, or that'll get warmed." Roughly translated, this means that Sid was going to spank Chessie's arse if he didn't get out of the pool.

On hearing this, Chessie just carried on cavorting and squealing like an excited pig, hoping Sid *would* carry out his threat on him. My nancy-boy cousin was full of beans on that day and had no intention of halting his behaviour, so Sid dragged him out of the water and kicked the shit out of him on the poolside. The children looked on in horror, and I'm sure several of the innocents are still receiving counselling to this day.

I once asked Chesswood if he'd ever held down a job. He informed me that he had worked in a sperm bank, but was sacked on his first day when he was caught drinking on the job!

I could never fathom Chesswood's deep desire for Mr Blewit who, at nearly seventy, resembled an old ruin. But as time marched on, I too fell deeply in love with an old ruin, called Roche Abbey.

Chapter 14

Roche Abbey

Secluded in a deep, misty valley on the outskirts of Maltby and surrounded by natural outcrops of magnesium limestone cliffs, lies the ruins of Roche Abbey. A visit to this magical place is a must for everyone. The abbey is approximately one and a half miles beyond Maltby and situated on lands occupying both sides of Maltby beck, or dyke, as we used to call it.

The joint founders of Roche Abbey were Richard de Busli and Richard Fitzturgis. Officially founded in 1147, its name reflects the rocky crags that encompass the ruined monastery. Monks from Newminster Abbey in Northumberland were sent to colonise this Cistercian monastery, and by the end of the 12th century, the mighty Norman and Gothic church as well as the majority of ancillary buildings were constructed.

The Dissolution of Monasteries by Henry VIII (1509-47) brought an abrupt end to the peaceful monastic lifestyle. At the time of the Dissolution in 1538, the Crown decided the fate of these buildings and all assets—but Maltby folk back then had their own ideas. The locals got together, decided that they had first claim on the abbey, and plundered its valuable artefacts, along with stones, lead and timber. (Well, Bonfire Night *was* coming up.)

If things looked bleak back then, they would look even bleaker when the lands on which the abbey sat came under the control of the 4th Earl of Scarborough and virtually disappeared off the face of the earth. To augment his family seat at Sandbeck,

Lord Scarborough commissioned Capability Brown in 1775 to renovate his estate, including the land on which the abbey lay. With no regard for the archaeological significance, Capability Brown flattened the remaining buildings, and with the skill and sensitivity of Britain's top landscape architect, turfed over the entire site. Bloody brilliant! I bet he was up all night dreaming that up. All he left standing, which remained not grassed over, were two transepts (rectangular space inserted between the apse and nave in the early Christian churches). On the upside, the one thing we do have to thank Brown for is the beautiful extensive woodlands and plethora of trees and shrubs he planted there.

Local legend says that Roche Abbey is haunted by a headless monk that roams the grounds at dusk. Stories of underground tunnels leading to hidden buildings and a lost wishing well are still talked about in school playgrounds around Maltby today. If you walk on the cliff footpath, which runs along the boundary of the grounds, you will be spellbound by the abbey's true beauty and tranquillity. It is breathtakingly spectacular. There is still a 13th century arched stone bridge that spans the beck, and the remaining enclosure walls of the church stand silent and serene—watching over the abbey, holding the painful secrets of its past in their stone hearts, remaining dignified and stoic to the onlooker.

I still feel the same now about Roche Abbey as I did as a child—completely overwhelmed and awestruck. It's a place I always think about when I am abroad or away from home. It's where my heart lies, trapped somewhere in time, hidden within the remaining stonework and grounds of the monastery.

You can walk to the abbey from the bottom of the crags, adjoining where the old the lido used to be sited. From here, you can wend your way through the woods with the beck on your right along a small footpath, which leads you straight into the abbey grounds. You have to pay now to actually enter the site, but it's still well worth it.

Around the grounds of the abbey, there are numerous horse chestnut trees *(Aesculus hippocasta-num)*, and come autumn, these are laden with their fruit, the mighty conker. Conker is the name given to the nut of the horse chestnut, and comes from the 19th century word *conker*, meaning "snail-shell". Conkers are also known as *obblyonkers* and *cheesers*. Apparently the first conker competition took place on the Isle of Wight in 1848. Prior to this, kids would use hazelnuts or snail shells. The fruit is a brown nut encased in a spiny green/brown shell.

To harvest the conkers, we would stand under-neath the chestnut trees and throw large sticks up into the massive domed crowns and their far reach-ing branches with the hope of knocking them off. What we never seemed to factor into this method of harvesting was that the great big sticks we were using to dislodge the conkers also came crashing down to earth. Added to this, we always went *conkering* in gangs and always stripped the same tree of its riches at the same time. It never occurred to us to split up and try different trees—after all, we were in a wood, and it was bloody full of them.

The sight and sound of huge falling pieces of wood and spiky green land mines careering down from the trees onto the unsuspecting ensemble below was verging on the ridiculous. Bruised and battered children with tear-stained faces and splinters the size of knitting needles embedded in their tiny bodies would joyfully hold aloft their prize conkers with the triumph and happiness of a football captain holding up his team trophy after a cup final. It was great to see one of your mates displaying his conker to the rest of the gang with the pride of a new father. Though the happiness would be whipped away in an instant when a descending lump of wood came crashing down, smashing their skulls open and rendering them unconscious.

Bigger gang members showed their bravado by scaling the gigantic trees in order to cherry-pick what looked like the biggest fruits. On one occasion, one gang member named Yam climbed high up into the tree's branches in search of a sizable conker, maybe to a height of twenty-five feet. Peering up into the foliage, he was barely visible to the boys at ground level.

We then heard him shout out loud, "I've spotted an absolute *corker*." Unfortunately, it was just beyond his reach at the end of a rickety branch, some twelve feet away from the main trunk. Yam was besotted with this particular conker, and again began enthusing about it to the congregation below, saying, "Wait till you see the size of this fucker."

By this time, the rest of the gang thought he was bullshitting and, ignoring the fact that he was still in the canopy of the tree, recommenced throwing sticks up at the conkers—and at him as well. Suddenly, we heard Yam squealing with delight. He'd obviously grasped his dream conker. What followed next was an almighty *crack* as the branch Yam was standing on snapped and broke away from the main body of the tree. Both Yam and the branch tumbled to earth, smashing off further boughs as they hurtled downwards towards the forest floor. The snapping of limbs and the *thud* of the crash-landing rocked the foundations of the ground where we were stood. With the concern of an absent father and the velocity of a bullet, the swarm of children at the base started frantically collecting the hundreds of conkers Yam's fall had dislodged. Not a thought was spared for our injured mate. We were obsessed with raking up this manna from heaven as quickly as our hands could move, stuffing the stash in our coat pockets like thieving little bastards.

Amazingly, Yam managed to come around and get to his feet, after what seemed like just seconds. *Bloody miracle,* I hear you saying to yourselves. It was only when he moved that we saw he had landed on one of the other gang members, who had nicely cushioned his fall. To make matters worse, we then ascertained that it was Yam's younger brother who had broken his fall. (Brotherly love? Or just wrong place at the wrong time?) Yam's sibling didn't seem to be moving, so Bones decided to piss on his face in order to help him come to.

Just as Bones was whipping out his tackle, Yam's brother murmured out to the now attentive crowd, "Did he get the big conker, then?"

This little kid was half dead, and his only concern was whether his big brother had got his prize conker. This memory was burnt onto my retina at that very moment in time. We all had a good old chin-wag about the incident at school the next day, and Yam proudly showed off his conker to the excited crowds who were gathered around him. It was, I have to say, an absolute beauty.

When you actually release a conker from its spiny case, the beautiful grain and magnificent colours are a sight to behold. The whole idea of collecting conkers was for the school competition held every October. It was totally unsupervised or even authorised by the school itself. The children organised the event, and anyone could take part.

Firstly, the conker is pierced with a knitting needle or nail straight through its centre, top to bottom. A piece of string or shoelace of about eighteen inches long is then carefully threaded through the hole, and a knot is tied at one end of the string—big enough so as to stop the conker from falling off when you swung it hard and fast. Your opponent would then hold his suspended conker in the air at arm's length for you to try and hit it with *your* conker. Each player takes it in turns to hit each other's conker. To hit the brown orb, you must hold the string in one hand, the conker held above it in the other hand. You swipe at the opponent's conker, letting go of your nut whilst still keeping hold of the string. The winner is the person whose conker remains intact and still on the string.

The actual aiming of your weapon and subsequent connection with the challenger's dangling conker left a lot to be desired. Kids would regularly have their knuckles rapped by a straying conker, its aim wide of the mark usually at great speeds, and I can vouch that this is a somewhat painful ordeal. If you were inadvertently whacked across the thumb or forefinger, you'd just grit your teeth, wait patiently for your turn, and reciprocate accordingly. Such was the fierceness of the competitions, people would also soak their conkers in vinegar and bake them in the oven to harden them up prior to the contests.

A brand new conker is referred to as a "none-er" (meaning it is worth no points). If you are played against a person whose conker had won six contests, and your conker had won three contests, the winner's conker would now be classed as a "ten-er" (6+3+1). It's a pity that children are not allowed to play conkers in schoolyards across the UK these days because of the killjoy health and safety extremists. What these arseholes don't realise is that they are robbing kids of their childhood. These excessive and over-the-top directives should be scrapped immediately. Children need to be exposed to certain rough and tumble games and sports so they are prepared for the dangerous world they are going to grow up in. Wrapping them in cotton wool and imposing strict regimes and guidelines is a complete load of bollocks. As a nation, we rank equal to Cambodia when it comes to major sporting achievements. However, we are currently the world champions at conkers (a fact worth noting).

The problem with the society we live in today (or the *Nanny state*, as it is often referred to), is that there are too many bloody do-gooders interfering and telling the rest of us what's right and what's wrong. I've spoken to thousands of people all around the globe, and whenever I ask them if they actually know any do-gooders, the answer is always a resounding "NO!" So, where the bloody hell are these people? If I do ever meet one, the first thing I'll do is rap him/her across the hands with my trusty conker to highlight what they are missing. And I think you will agree with me—that'll show 'em who's bloody right.

When I was growing up, the gang and I would think nothing of getting up at six in the morning, meeting down on the bottom field at five past, then venturing out for the whole day, and arriving back home at eight that evening. Our parents hadn't got a bloody clue where we were and didn't know or bother about who we'd been with—or a thought given as to whether or not we had eaten. We just fended for ourselves and got on with life. The fact that we didn't eat much at home and all resembled scrawny little runts meant we didn't feel a constant need for food, like children of today do. Obesity in kids was something of a rarity back then, and when a kid had a bag of sweets or an apple, he always shared his goodies with the other gang members.

Kids just lived on life itself. It was a case of having to. No one was around to complain to, and when they were, they didn't listen. Crimes against children did occur, and in certain cases, were just as horrific as we hear about today. But televisions and blanket media coverage, highlighting and brainwashing people, hadn't really kicked off in the 60s. And if you actually had a television set, you were either considered rich, or had a family member who was a top cat burglar.

And while I'm on the subject of brainwashing, I was advised recently that I should use the correct terminology—that being *cranial-cleansing*. What a complete bag of bollocks. I recently came across another politically correct viewpoint when I used the word "brainstorming". I was accused of taking for granted that people had brains. The term I was told to adopt was "thought shower," which sounds like something you would do in a porn movie! On hearing this, I suggested a few rather apt words for the sage who was lecturing me at the time, these being: "Tosser," "Wanker," "Gob-shite," "Wassack," "Nob-head," and "Twat"—all of which can be found in the Oxford English Dictionary and all extremely descriptive and relevant to my adviser, who will remain nameless. But you know who you are, Mr Dagless of Rawmarsh.

Chapter 15

Fishing at Langold Lake

For my ninth birthday, Mum reluctantly bought Craig and me each a fishing rod. Most of the kids I knew were into angling, so we were both excited about the prospect of going to Langold Lake and testing out our tackle. Langold is about five miles from Maltby and one mile from Oldcotes, heading towards Worksop. The village was built to house the miners of nearby Costhorpe Colliery, which along with nearly all the rest of the pits in the UK, is now closed. Maltby still has a working mine, but for how much longer, no one knows.

Unlike its nearby towns and villages, Langold does boast a large lake, which was the nearest we got to pretending that we had the sea in our vicinity. Adjacent to the lake, there used to be an open air lido, and opposite this looming out of the lake itself, was a three-tiered diving platform. When I was a boy, several young men drowned in the lake, due to its strong undercurrents and masses of submerged pondweed. None of my mates dared venture into the murky depths, and we all treated the lake with a fearful respect.

One evening, after a great deal of deliberation, the mates and me decided to *wag*, play truant, from school the following day and go fishing at the lake instead. A quick-fire plan was hatched, and a rendez-vous set up. Fishing tackle was stowed away in our makeshift den that night so we could hit the road running the next day without our parents becoming suspicious. Looking back now, I have to smile to myself, realising just how thick we were. Firstly, we normally got up for school at seven most mornings, but on this particular day, due to the five-mile walk and the prospect of catching some dawn tench and skimmer bream, we sneaked out of our sacks at four. So by four-fifteen we were out of the door and away.

What part of not being at the table for breakfast with the rest of the family didn't we understand? Coupled with this fact, our mums actually used to escort us on our journey to school every day. I remember that at this particular juncture in my education, we were heavily into studying history and geography. Because more things were continually happening, history was much harder, so we had to remember more. Geography on the other hand seemed somewhat easier—due to rising sea levels causing more places to disappear and less actual places to study.

School was never my favourite place so the proposition of a day out fishing was a no-brainer for me.

Laden to the hilt with fishing tackle and bait, six pairs of legs made their weary way out of Maltby, past Roche Abbey, and into Oldcotes—a journey of about four miles. Here, we caught our breath and rested awhile. Just as we were about to forge on and turn right towards Langold, Webbo piped up that he needed to take a dump and asked his fellow anglers if anyone had brought along toilet paper. A resounding "No" rang out from the crowd so he decided a large dock leaf would suffice. Dock grew everywhere and was excellent for easing the pain of nettle stings on the skin. (The jury is still out on the aspect of arse wiping.) He unshackled his gear, quickly removed his *kecks* and undies, and squatted down behind an isolated bush in a nearby garden. Just as the tortoise head popped out (as the shit made its way into the world), a booming voice broke the silence of the morning air.

"What the chuffing hell do you think you're doing, sonny-boy?" said a ruddy-faced man from his upstairs opened window.

"I stung my arse on a clump of nettles earlier, and I'm rubbing a dock leaf on it for relief," replied Webbo.

"How the bleeding hell did you sting your arse?" the man went on to say, fleetingly amused by the lad's obvious predicament.

"When I was having a shit just now," Webbo responded rather quizzically.

The man's face went from pillar-box red to vermillion so we collectively grabbed Webbo's tackle and scurried off in the direction of the lake, leaving our mate to clear up the mess, so to speak.

We arrived at our destination twenty minutes later, and as we looked over the water, our jaws dropped in total awe. Wreathes of steam and smoke seemed to dance on the surface and rise a short distance before disappearing into the drier air above. The lake was silent and still. The only noise was that of coots *(Fulica atra)*, small waterfowl renowned for their aggressive and territorial squabbles with each other, punctuating the low-lying spirals of mists in short outbursts. Their echoes bounced off the wall at the head of the lake like intermittent sound of gunfire and then disappeared as they were reabsorbed back into the mist shrouding the mere. The sun was struggling with all its might to punch its way through the morning cloud cover, and the water resembled liquid mercury in its ripple-like state, gently lapping against the bank side in a waking haze. The scene was set for a good day's fishing.

The sport of angling dates back years and gets ever more popular with new clubs springing up every week around the country. Back then, fishing as we now know it was in its infancy. I am amazed at the diversity of baits and lures used today by anglers in the hope of capturing their intended prey. Halibut paste, cat meat, dog biscuits, luncheon meat, boilies, peanuts, tiger bread, and sweetcorn—the list is endless. If these baits had been around in my child-hood, the only place I would have been lucky enough to see them would have been on my bloody dinner plate on Sundays!

All we used back then were maggots and worms. Reel specifications now include "centre pin," "ball race," "bait runner," "rear drag," "wipe your arse," and "suck you off" features, whilst rods have become enormous lightweight power poles, reinforced with super lithium, and with integral elastics, power tops, and cupping tips. We used to fish with split cane or fibreglass rods. I remember one of the lads taking bread to use as bait, hoping to catch roach and rudd. He hadn't got to the end of the street before we'd all stripped him of his Hovis, and devoured the lot. He should have known better and used his own loaf before bringing this veritable feast with him. There was no way ducks and fish were having spare bread, when we were all starving hungry. What was he thinking, the bloody muppet?

Generally, before embarking upon any new pursuit or hobby, they say it's wise to seek advice and knowledge of your chosen subject. *Bollocks to that for a game of soldiers*. We just made it up as we went along and muddled through the best we could. Advice was never sought, and such was our impetu-osity and short-sightedness, that if freely given, was completely ignored. It was a competition with our gang to see who could tackle up and commence *splodging* (fishing) first. Our preparation was shambolic, our tackle decrepit, and our skills nonexistent. All in all, we were a complete shower of shit. It's no wonder we hardly ever caught anything.

On one occasion, we actually accused the lake bailiff of not putting the fish that had been caught the previous day back into the lake in order that one of our gang could catch it. We'd sit for hours, staring at the tops of our floats, praying and hoping that a huge fish would pull it under and take our bait.

It might have been helpful if on my first three fishing trips I'd actually attached a maggot or indeed, anything to the end of my hook. No one bothered to mention this small, significant detail to me. My mates were bastards when it came to sharing vital information like this. Eventually we all grasped the basics, and a true love of the sport captured us all for life. The miracle happens when you land your first big fish. A relationship with angling then grips you like a fever and never lets go.

Having spent three hours tackling up, I was finally fishing. My bait for the day was earthworms. I'd dug up hundreds of these fat, juicy creatures from our vegetable patch before I retired to bed the previous night. The problem with worms, though, is that they refuse to stay still whilst you are trying to skewer them onto your hook. (How inconsiderate of them.) Having threaded the oversized barbed hook through my finger twice, I decided to change my bait to maggots, as they were relatively easy in comparison. As I reached for my bait box, somehow my worm had hooked itself. I was astounded and equally pissed off that a dumb worm could achieve this feat in seconds. I had been struggling for an eternity and Mr *Lumbricus Terrestris* had snared itself with one nifty wriggle. With bait finally secured, all I had to do was release the bail arm on my reel and expertly cast my line just beyond the reeds to where I intended to fish. What could possibly go wrong?

With the skill of a complete twat coupled with a sharp gust of wind, I launched my bait skywards, only to find that the hook had firmly lodged itself in my right earlobe. To compound matters, the worm reluctantly managed to stay secured on the end of my hook and quickly made for the safety of my ear hole. At this stage of the game I decided not to draw any attention to my plight and spare myself from further embarrassment and humiliation.

With an insouciant air, I snipped the line off just below the hook and retackled my rig again—only this time, my bait of choice was maggots. Trying to retrieve a sharp, barbed hook from your ear is no easy task. Unfortunately the worm freed itself and was on its way westwards to meet my brain. The hook had managed to totally penetrate my earlobe, and I noticed a droplet of blood on my finger. Ginner strolled up to see if I'd caught anything and suddenly noticed my new earpiece.

In a more manly tone than he normally used, he said, "What's that all about, you numpty?"

"Oh, I thought I'd start wearing an earring like big Wacker in the village," I replied.

Big Wacker was the local heavy, and no one messed with him. He'd recently had his ear pierced, and it quickly became cool to follow his lead. He was a fashion icon, and everyone was scared shitless of him.

"Yeah, it looks okay, but if I were you, I'd have a proper one. You look a proper twat with that fish-hook in your lughole," Ginner went on.

At this, I carried on my pretence of concentrating on the fishing and inadvertently twiddled my new earpiece, getting the barb of the hook embedded in my forefinger. I honestly think that I was put onto this earth to show the rest of mankind how *not* to do things. As luck would have it, Ginner didn't notice and moved on.

At long last, I was actually fishing—tackled up, baited up, and in the exact spot I intended to be in. Life was beginning to look up. Suddenly, like a bolt from the blue, there was an almighty splash to the left of my float. This caused a mini tidal wave to lap over my feet, which were dangling off the jetty, just hovering over the skin of the mere.

What the bleeding hell was that? I thought to myself, swiftly removing my legs from the water surface. *Could it be the fearsome Langold pike?* I wondered. The pike was reputed to be in the region of fifty pounds and was said to have eaten an unsuspecting Labrador who happened to be swimming in the reeds near to the lake side.

I rapidly turned around to see if any of my fellow anglers had witnessed this spectacle. Looming over me like Frankenstein's monster, Webbo was doubled up with laughter.

"Did you see that?" I said, horror chiselled into my startled expression.

"Yes, I did. It was me. You didn't answer me when I asked you for some maggots so I took it on myself to attract your attention by throwing your flask of soup into the water," said Webbo.

The one thing I loved about my mates was their logic and reasoning. Throw your mate's lunch into the lake and deprive him of both food and fish all day. It's bloody priceless when you think about it.

Sometimes Webbo could be something of a prick. It was pretty obvious to me that any fish who had inadvertently wandered into my particular area had now pissed off for good. The sight and sound of my large thermos flask hitting the water like a depth charge was enough to ruin my day's fishing.

With a heavy heart and having lost the will to live, I reeled in then decided to try one last cast to see if I could salvage something. A mighty minnow would have sufficed. I drew my arms back and, with all the strength I could muster, propelled my bait into the centre of the lake. For a split second, I felt delighted with my efforts, and then I saw a white spear hurtling like an arrow through the air, with my float and hook attached! When I looked down between my legs I discovered that my rod had shrunk from twelve feet to three. The top two sections had parted company with the butt handle. I never intended to spearfish and can still picture in my mind's eye the rod speeding through the air like a javelin, never to see the light of day again.

I reluctantly tackled down and left my mates still fishing. Crestfallen and feeling sorry for myself, I trudged back home via the school. One of my classmates happened to be walking through the school gates and called out to me, asking where I had been all day. Horrified, I realised that school was just finishing and, in the corner of my eye, spotted my Mum standing in the playground, looking like Attila the Hun. I had to think quickly in order to stem the flow of her anger. I sneakily crept around the perimeter fencing and, with the stealth of a cat, climbed on top of one of the terrapin classroom structures annexed off the main school building. But as I clambered onto the flat roof, I slipped and banged my head, causing a huge egg to develop. As I came to my senses, I heard Mum and the headmaster calling me to come down. Slowly I descended, still a little dazed and bewildered.

"What the bloody hell have you been doing up there? And come to think of it, where the chuffing hell have you been all day?" barked my irate mother.

"I left home early this morning to retrieve my tennis ball from the roof of the classroom, and the last thing I remember is falling and banging my head," was my feeble reply. After all, the evidence of my injury was there for the entire world to see.

"Have you been stuck on that roof all day then?" my mother added, incredulously.

"I must have been. I really can't remember," I said.

"Well you look a little dishevelled and spaced out. I believe you, but thousands wouldn't. Sounds a bit fishy to me," she retorted.

I hobbled home, joyful in the fact that she had fallen for my tale—hook, line, and sinker.

Chapter 16

Grannies and Ghoulies

Great Grandma McCloud was one of the best tellers of ghost stories I ever had the pleasure to listen to. Well into her 80s and a trifle frail on her pins, she could spin a yarn that would make the hairs on your neck stand up. Such was her vocal dexterity she had us spellbound and teetering on the edge of terror whenever she imparted one of her tales about ghosts and spectres. Granny McCloud lived the story she was telling, through her eyes and facial expressions—as well as her facial hair. If you have ever been in the company of a person who is profoundly interesting and charismatic, you find yourself totally absorbed in their world. This is called *deep listening*—when you are silent and fixated on your narrator, listening to every word they say. When Granny related an anecdote, we were bewitched and under her spell.

One winter night, I happened to stumble on Granny Mac, as we often referred to her. She made her way home through the alley near where she resided.

"Walk with me, sonny, and I'll treat you to a hot beverage and a good tale," she said, her eyes widening even more as she spoke, her lips curling witchlike, as if she were about to burst into an evil cackle.

The tea sounded great, and the inevitable ghost story was a bonus, as I was suffering from constipation at the time, and it seemed like the perfect remedy. We arrived at her abode and, in no time at all, were sitting in front of a roaring fire in her spotless cobbled kitchen, cradling the warmth of the mugs in our cupped hands. The only sound was that of the *tick-tock* of the grandfather clock in the hall, letting us know in its own mechanical way that time was slowly passing.

Just as Granny Mac was about to begin her evening's entertainment, the back door to the kitchen blew wide open causing smoke to cascade back down the chimney and into the room. Granny never flinched and coolly asked me to get up and secure the door. This I did at lightning speed, mainly due to the fact that as the door sprung open in my startled state, I had managed to spill my red hot tea onto my testicles! Stepping outside to cool my nuts down a fraction, I noticed the night sky had darkened and, from the bottom of the garden, heard the rustle of dead leaves.

"That's your dead great-grandfather saying goodnight to me," Granny explained.

I was back in my chair as fast as a rat runs up a drainpipe, door secured, tea in hand—but bollocks still on fire. I must admit that I was somewhat taken aback by the acuteness of Granny's hearing, regarding the rustling of the leaves, and slightly bemused by the fact that my great-grandfather was still alive, though he'd left her twenty years ago for the postman. Maybe she knew something I didn't—or my great-grandfather was *branching out*!

Finally, she began to tell me about her cousin Helen, who had been blind since birth. She lived in a small village near Doncaster in the 1920s. Being blind, Helen struggled through her school years and subsequently became a loner. She lived on a farm, and her job was to deliver the churns of fresh milk to the local dairy. This journey was twelve miles round trip, and her mode of transport was a horse and cart.

Helen would set off every morning at the crack of dawn so the milk would be at its freshest.

After making her delivery, she occasionally took a detour and visited her widowed aunt in the next village where she would spend the day keeping her company. Helen's horse had travelled this same path for years, and instinctively knew the route, including the detour. Helen had a special bond with her horse and cared deeply for her aunt. They were the two things in her life that really mattered to her. Following supper, Helen would make her way back home, her passage taking her through an isolated wooded copse. It was here in this copse some ten years earlier that a young girl had been mutilated and murdered. Not knowing this fact, Helen was both unaware and unaffected by the tragedy.

One moonless night as Helen was heading towards the copse, her horse suddenly stopped. Helen felt a person clamber onto the cart with what seemed like a small case and sit next to her. She could feel the heavy corner of the case on her leg, and smelled the sweet fragrance of leather in the night air. No words were spoken, but due to her blindness, all Helen's other senses were heightened and finely tuned. She felt safe and realised that this stranger meant her no harm. The person then gently took hold of Helen's hand, and from the softness of the touch, Helen realised that it was a girl.

After approximately one mile, the horse came to an abrupt halt. They had arrived at the wooded copse. A shiver went down Helen's spine, and the girl's grip on her hand dramatically increased in pressure. Through her touch, Helen could feel the pain and suffering of the stranger being transmitted, and experienced a deep sadness and loss the likes of which she had never felt before. Helen could not sense the presence of anyone or anything other than that of the girl. She knew from her grip on the reins that the horse was calm and placid indicating there was no impending danger. She reassured the girl that everything was going to be all right, told her not to be afraid and that whatever was frightening the girl, causing her to suffer, would cease.

Helen then suddenly felt the girl's hand relax and drop away. The cart rocked as the stranger dismounted with her package, and the horse nodded its head several times, needing Helen to steady it. Helen could still sense the presence of the girl and beckoned that she should return onto the cart. Without warning, a loud and powerful gust of wind roared through the night air, and the stranger was gone. Helen called out to the girl in vain, but her cries were lost to the sound of the wind. Before she could rationalise what had just happened and come to terms with the situation, the horse calmly began to move forward. Helen was filled with a sense of emptiness. Something felt like it was missing, and she couldn't fathom what it was.

When she got home, she relayed the story of the stranger to her father who went on to explain to Helen what had happened in the copse some ten years earlier. He said that she should be more vigilant and discourage all strangers. Helen conveyed to her father that the stranger in question was a young girl and meant her no harm, but her father had spoken and wouldn't listen to another word on the subject. Helen went to bed that evening feeling somewhat bemused and frustrated.

The following week, Helen was travelling the same route home, heading towards the copse again. At the exact same point of her previous outing, her horse stopped. Just as before, Helen felt the stranger climb onto the cart and sit beside her, again taking hold of her hand. No words were spoken, and when the cart reached the copse, the exact same scenario reoccurred. The stranger disappeared into the night, leaving Helen feeling disheartened. When Helen felt compelled to tell her father about the incident, he decided to accompany her on the next trip.

The following week, Helen again made the same journey, only this time with her father. Again, approximately one mile from the copse, the horse brought the cart to a sudden halt. Helen then requested that her father dismount in order for her stranger to climb on board. Helen's father found her demands somewhat unreasonable, but decided to comply with them and duly alighted. He would walk behind the horse and cart in order to monitor the situation. To her father, everything looked completely normal, but Helen could sense and feel her stranger, just as she had on the previous two trips. They arrived at the copse, and without instruction, the horse stopped. Helen's father was several yards behind the cart and had decided to bring closure to the night's proceedings. He had witnessed absolutely nothing. No person, no case— nothing! It had been a total fiasco and a complete waste of his time.

Suddenly and unexpectedly, a fierce, howling wind ripped through the trees and knocked Helen's father to the ground. The horse reared up and galloped forwards, unseating Helen in the process and smashing the side of the cart into one of the nearby trees. Helen's father got to his feet and rushed over to where Helen lay. In her outstretched hand, she was holding a small suitcase. Helen was motionless, and her frantic father feared the worst. As he caressed her bloodied face and kissed her forehead, Helen whispered to him, in her dying breath, to open the case. With tear-stained eyes, he obeyed his daughter's last wishes. He unclasped her small fingers from the handle of the case and opened it.

Now at this stage of Granny Mac's story, I was on the point of shitting myself. Not daring to move or flinch, and with mouth agog and eyes as wide as saucers, I was rigid with anticipation.

"What do you think he found when he opened the case, sonny?" Granny said to me.

"I don't know," was my humble reply.

"A girl's leg," said my Granny.

"A girl's leg?" I replied in total shock and horror.

"Yes, a girl's leg. Just like the one I'm pulling now, Warren. Look how late it is. You'd better piss off quickly or you'll be in for a beating."

Well, what a complete nasty bastard my conniving Granny Mac is, I thought.

I had been hooked on every sodding word of the story and believed it without question. The old coot had been lying through her false teeth and ripping the piss out of me. What type of a scheming witch would do such a thing to a small, innocent boy? What kind of ancient trout would scare a lad senseless and derive such pleasure in making him late home so he would get a thrashing?

On the way out, I had one last question for her.

"Why did you refer to me as Warren?" (The fact that she associated me with having a leg like a girl was okay, but I took umbrage with the name *Warren*.)

"Warren idiot!" was her swift reply.

Chapter 17

Little Rivers

Being born into working class stock automatically made our family poor—a prerequisite of being a proletarian. Needless to say, having no money meant we had to create our own entertainment. I have poignant memories of being hungry, and being skint was the norm—after all, every other kid I played with was in the same boat. But I did have a couple of qualities I could boast about: an abundance of audacity and spirit. I wasn't deliberately naughty as a child and never intended causing anyone undue pain or heartache, but I was tempestuous and mildly insane.

When I think of the ways we now mollycoddle our children and strive to reward them for actually getting out of bed on Saturday mornings before eleven, I quickly reflect back to my childhood and think that I'd have been out playing on the fields for the best part of five hours by then. I don't entirely blame parents for the quandary they face with their children's upbringing, but kids of today seem to get everything they want. Parents can't and don't punish their offspring in case they are hauled in front of the magistrates and prosecuted for child abuse. Kids have the upper hand—and what's frightening is, they know it! This makes for a society where rules don't matter, and a disproportionate amount of blame is placed on the victim and not the criminal. We are berated for standing up for justice and wanting proper measures put in place to deter criminals once and for all.

I was never a criminal myself, and the only mischief I got up to was the occasional scrap with another lad. Whenever I got into a fight or an argument as a nipper, it was a case of "May the best man win," simple as that. We never relied on guns or knives—or indeed drugs. We just tooled up with our basic homemade metal knuckle dusters and sniffed petrol out of Webbo's dad's motorcycle tank for good measure. We would improvise during the battles and altercations and use anything that came to hand, like soil in the eyes, a large brick to the back of the head, stinging nettles to the face, etc. If you did pulverise your opponent, you would have the decency to help them to their feet and thank them for being a first class sport. You would then, and *only* then, give them a really good kick up the arse to merrily send them on their way.

The best part of actually winning the fights was the drama that followed; not quite being economical with the truth, or blatant lying. When it comes to lying, it is worth remembering that it takes two to lie—one to lie, and one to listen! The bigger the actual lie, the better the story. If you lost a scrap, the best thing you could do was to quickly forget about it and graciously let your mates ridicule you for the next few days. It was no good whinging or protesting about it, or you would be labelled by your peers as a "mardy arse" or a "maungy bastard," both derogatory terms used for moaners. Worse still, if you hadn't put up a decent performance in the brawl and fought like a "nancy boy" or "sissy" (terms used to describe gay and girlie characteristics), you were called such names as "bum chum," "iron hoof," or "piccalilli weasel". The latter was in fact the precursor to the term "chutney ferret". All these names were associated with being a social leper and an outcast. Kids could and still can be cruel and are not concerned with discrimination or character assassination. This was known as *street language* in the 60s, and everyone used it whether it offended or not, as the case may be. So, if you're going to tell a lie about winning or losing a battle, always make sure it's a good one!

Mining families breed hardy stock, with brawn always outweighing brains. Most of us suffered from being asinine and it was expected that the only way to expunge this was through education. The obstacle we faced here was that to obtain an education, we had to attend school. At this point the theory went tits up, because we didn't like school back then and missed it at every opportunity. There were far more important issues to deal with, like *ratting* and *river hopping*.

Maltby beck, or dyke, was where our gang would frequent on a regular basis, usually at weekends. This tree-lined stream provided entertainment and wildlife packed into one. The dyke was approximately six feet wide and about a foot deep. The water was somewhat murky, and the only marine life it supported were minnows, (surprisingly, the smallest members of the carp family), and bullheads, (a solitary fish found underneath stones). Also known as "miller's-thumb," bullheads are spiny, broad-headed freshwater fish that can wound you if handled incorrectly.

We'd buy a small fishnet from Milnes, the local store, to catch our intended monsters—none of which grew to more than three inches long. We'd then adapt a jam jar by piercing the metal lid with two holes, through which a piece of string was threaded. By tying two knots at each end and firmly securing the lid to the string, we could carry the jar when the top was screwed on. It was then a case of filling the jar with water and catching the said fish, which allowed

126

us to proudly parade and display them to the rest of the world.

From our house to the Beck was about one mile. By the time I had reached home, invariably, all the fish were dead due to a total lack of oxygen—and a total lack of water! I always made the holes in the lid too wide, and in my excitement never properly secured the top of the jam jar, therefore spilling all the liquid from my container. Hence, the fish died. I never seemed to learn from this simple, elementary error and went on to commit the same idiotic mistake over and over again. I must have murdered thousands of the little bastards over the years and found it inexplicable as to why they were dead. I have always been impetuous, excitable, and hasty in my decision-making... or have I? I never seem to be able to read instructions thoroughly or indeed plan anything. I just fly by the seat of my pants, usually with disastrous consequences. Having no patience is not a good attribute for fishing, but I still do it, to other anglers' annoyance.

Another great pursuit of happiness we would thoroughly enjoy down at the beck was swinging. And no, I don't mean swapping partners for sexual gratification. Ginner would provide the gang with a large coil of rope, usually in the region of twenty feet long, for the purpose of building a rope swing over the stream. The rope was always of excellent quality, and approximately one inch thick. You could have pulled a Sherman tank with it—such was its tensile strength. We would locate a suitable tree growing next to the brook, and being the best tree climber in our gang, I was the one tasked to skim up it and attach the rope to a substantial branch of the tree.

With the heavy rope draped over my neck and shoulders, I would carefully make my way up the main trunk until I reached an appropriate limb, which normally grew parallel to the stream at a height of about twelve feet above ground level. With legs firmly clamped around the branch, coupled with the balance of an acrobat, I would quickly lash the rope to the bough. Once it was firmly secured, I would descend via the rope. The only problem with this way of coming back down to earth was that when I eventually reached *terra firma*, I always ended up knee-deep in water, plumb-bang in the centre of the stream. All the planning up to the descent was carried out to perfection, but the actual landings were disastrous.

Once again, I would commit the same mistakes over and over. It would have been nice if on just one occasion, I could have illustrated to my peers that I did possess a modicum of intelligence by actually learning from my numerous reoccurring errors. This never seemed to be the case though, because when excitement kicked in, my rationale and common sense disappeared. It's still the same for me today. When I was finally retrieved from the water, I adjusted the rope accordingly, and then formed a slip knot at the end. Through this knot was fed a short, solid metal bar, two feet long and one inch thick. (This was in effect the part we sat on, with legs dangling down either side.)

When constructing a rope swing, choosing the actual site was of paramount importance. It had to be near a large section of riverbank so the launch or takeoff could be accomplished with relative ease. We also had to ensure that there was sufficient space around the tree with no hidden obstacles or snags in order to minimise injury when taking flight or landing. It was also vital that the other side of the stream had to be inspected and approved by all gang members for when we carried out "plummet drops".

These were achieved by swinging across the dyke at great speeds and waiting until the rope had reached the point or arc that it could go no farther. At this precise summit, we would then release hold of the rope and plummet like a stone back down to earth. This operation was usually carried out onto unsuspecting kids who happened to be on the other side of the river bank. When you landed on them from a great height and smashed them to the ground, it made rope-swinging seem all the more worthwhile—like it had a proper purpose.

Another technique used was *backies* or *taxis*, which were performed by kids jumping onto the backs of other children who were already on the swing whilst it was in full motion, thus propelling both parties in unison. Timing here was critical. The squeals of laughter and happiness emanating from kids swinging over the river, either singularly or in taxi mode, spitting on their audience below—and in Bones's case, pissing—was a scene to behold. Experience taught us to be extra vigilant when observing rope-swinging from close quarters. We would spend hours swinging to and fro over the beck, getting piss wet through and bruised to buggery—but we loved every minute of it.

Almost as wide as he was high, a lad called Clarkey moved onto our street and decided that it was his God-given right to take over the leadership of our gang. And there was very little we could do about it, due to his gargantuan frame. He was built like a gladiator, or like a "brick shithouse," as we used to say—and we didn't want to mess with him. One day he just turned up, and by the next day he was in charge. Clarkey was a chronic bad-mouther–basically he was a bumptious twat who bullied us at every opportunity. No one liked him, but we did revere his throwing skills down at the beck.

Clarkey hated rats with a passion, and the beck was full of them. What none of us knew at the time was the rodents we were hunting down at the beck were in fact water voles *(Arvicola terrestris)*, which are vegetarians and cause no harm to anyone or anything. Their downfall is that they resemble rats and are often mistakenly referred to as *Water Rats.*

Clarkey's hatred stemmed from being bitten by a brown, or common rat *(Rattus norvegicus)*, when he was searching for birds eggs in a small fissure in a rocky outcrop on the crags. When he retrieved his hand from within the hole, the rat was still firmly clamped onto his index finger and wouldn't let go. Screaming in pain and scared shitless, he ran fifty yards for help with the rat still locked onto his digit. It was only when he tripped over a protruding root that the offending rodent released its grip. To make matters worse, when Clarkey hit the ground, he managed to knock one of his front teeth out—so you can understand and empathise with his loathing of these furry creatures.

Rats have a bad reputation for the economical destruction they cause to the countryside and are classed as undesirable vermin because of their association with diseases. Clarkey wasn't in the least bit concerned with their reputation. He was just pissed off with the fact that he was missing a top front molar, and it made him look even more comical than he did before. It also hindered his speech, making him more self-conscious and even more of a bully.

The equipment used on the ratting expeditions was usually catapults and a pocket full of marbles, simple as that. In Clarkey's case, however, this extended to a sack full of "half charlies," which were wall bricks that had been broken in two. Trying to grasp even a large brick when you are a child is hard enough, but actually being able to throw one accurately was a blooming miracle. Clarkey could perform such miracles because he possessed hands the size of shovels and had the eyesight of a hawk. This combination proved lethal—and if Clarkey missed with his aim, six other lads would be ready in the wings, catapults loaded and ready to fire.

The silly fat water voles had no chance. We would hear a *plop* in the water, and see the fur ball swimming across the beck to the safety of its bank side burrow, head aloft, and cruising steadily. On Clarkey's command, the target would be blitzed with large bricks and a hail of marbles. It was pure carnage. When Clarkey took a vole out, he obliterated it. He very rarely needed the backup of the glass balls as he was such a crack shot. I had the toilsome task of being Clarkey's caddy when it came to carrying his ammo, and it weighed a bloody tonne.

When Clarkey was in action, he was a man on a mission. He had a severe method of exterminating his prey, which worked effectively for him. He had no intention of crippling or maiming his victims. Clarkey's intention was to cause instant death. Fortuitously, along the banks of the dyke, there was a proliferation of voles, and copious amounts of bricks and marbles. His scintillating displays of brick throwing, coupled with his accuracy of shot, made him a deadly foe for the voles. He would take enormous pleasure from his lethal actions and notch his walking stick after every kill. There were so many nicks out of his stick that after a few years it collapsed when he was leaning on it, resulting in him losing his other front tooth on the capping of a wall. (I think between the rats and the wall bricks, the balance was somewhat restored regarding Clarkey's teeth, or lack of them.)

Just down from the village of Hooton Levitt, the beck split off into several smaller streams, which were known locally as the Little Rivers. It was here that I was schooled in another watery pursuit—the art of river jumping—from an accomplished lad named Briels who had a transcendent skill for leaping. Due to the topography of the land, the stream branched out like extended fingers for about one hundred yards before it reunited all its watery tentacles and became one again. Between each little river, the ground was marshy, with sections of quicksand that could suck you down to your waist with ease. It was a dangerous place to play, and to jump the streams you had to have a sound knowledge of where to leap and where to land.

Briels, being somewhat older than the rest of the gang, was in the enviable position of being taller and more agile than the rest of us. Watching this boy hurdling the streams, catlike and elegant, never putting a foot wrong, and all at great speed was a sight to cherish. His balance and poise was as good as that of a prize boxer, and the way he could spring into the air, land on one leg, and then launch himself back into the atmosphere from the same leg was magnificent. He was nimble and quick-footed and knew exactly which sections of the rivers were passable and which were not. He had the crafts of a river ghillie, and we always followed his lead.

Jumping over rivers littered with pockets of quicksand may not be everyone's cup of tea, and as a parent, I would be mortified if I thought my children were playing in such a dangerous place. Looking back, I now realise that this sport was probably not one of the safest games I ever took part in. And in hindsight, I should never have gone there. The problem, though, was Briels. Unfortunately for us, he was tough, possessed more muscles, chided us, and called us "puffs" if we didn't go with him. No one liked to be labelled a puff, even though back then, its connotation was associated with being "girlie" rather than a "receiver of swollen goods."

Briels was basically a bully, but so were most of the older kids to their younger and smaller siblings. Bullying was part of life, and no matter what you said to your parents or elders, it was simply passed off and ignored. The attitude back then was, *Stop moaning and sort it out yourself.* It was horrendous for some kids, who were mentally and physically scarred for life. Teachers, police, parents, and indeed, anyone in a position of authority didn't take it seriously enough to stop it. We were reconciled to our fate and had to sort it out in our own way.

Bullies threatened and dissuaded us from notifying anyone, usually meaning elders and parents, of our situation. When bullies dished out their mean tricks, they were never part of a fraternity or gang—they were just individuals who caused people pain and distress. Brotherhoods were made up of members who looked out for each other and protected their friends and brothers. As a bully you were alienated, and never really accepted in a proper gang. Bullies were tolerated, but never really befriended. When a gang member was singled out for torment or picked upon, that same gang member would only report his plight to other gang members. Following on from this, all the brotherhood would meet up in secret and decide on an appropriate course of action.

On one such occasion, Craig was getting singled out and bullied by a lad known as Tabs. Craig called a secret meeting down in the "bullring" to explain his predicament to the assembled Council, and form a plan.

Now Tabs was somewhat older than the rest of us and a great deal bigger. But he was only one lad, and we were six. As evening fell and shadows lengthened, we stalked Tabs from a safe distance, monitoring his every move from our hidden vantage point. When dusk became darkness, we slipped on our balaclavas to conceal our identities and tooled up with broom handles, which had been sawn in half, ready for action. When Tabs ventured into the "snicket" (a small alleyway connecting two streets), we pounced on him. The ferocity of the blows that rained down on him, along with the kicks to his body, were frightening, but he had started this particular fight, and that night, we ended it. Tabs could only speculate on the identity of his attackers, but he never bullied Craig or indeed any other member of our gang again. I'm not saying that the course of action we doled out to Tabs was right, but neither was bullying, and what we did that night was effective in putting an end to the abuse.

Another bully who crossed swords with our gang was a lad known as Weasel Face. He was a wrong 'un, and delighted in causing undue pain and suffering to other children. He once picked on Webbo for no apparent reason other than the fact that he was much smaller, had ginger hair, and supposedly glowered at him. Weasel Face threatened Webbo and then bad mouthed our gang. This really pissed us off. We held our secret meeting and redressed the balance with Weasel Face as we did with Tabs. But to add insult to injury, I farted on his tongue to give him a taste of his own medicine! On the topic of wrongs being righted, I only wish I could dish out this kind of retribution now on my neighbour, for pissing through my letter box.

Chapter 18

Apple Scrumping at Granny Fart's

At the far end of Maltby, going west towards Rotherham, sat a lovely ancient apple orchard owned by a lady known as "Granny Fart". The produce of this fine orchard was ripe for picking and nicking (scrumping or stealing) in the autumn months, and our gang always obliged. We were regular uninvited visitors with a mission to pilfer as many apples as we could carry. We always scrumped in coats which had "poacher's pockets" in the inside lining so would could hide and hold more fruit. I know that stealing should not be glorified, and it is indeed a crime—but there's something about raiding apple and pear orchards that still gives me a thrill to this day. I can't fully explain or indeed contain my excitement when swiping apples. I do love the taste of a fresh, crunchy, hard, sour apple and I do get a buzz from being in someone else's garden and stealing their fruit. But other than the added fact of getting aroused down below in the nether regions, I am somewhat at a loss as to why I actually thieve apples.

Where the name Granny Fart derived from is anyone's guess, but when I had the unfortunate and terrifying experience of being in her close proximity, the smell of shit did spring to mind. She was a hoary, venerable old trout with a violent temper that also happened to be a pot shot with a gun. I remember standing behind her in the fish and chip shop when she was complaining to the owner, Mr Blewit. She asked if the fish she had just purchased was dead—as she thought it had eaten most of her chips.

Her favourite words were "How much?" This proved two things: firstly, she was a skinflint, and secondly, she was from Yorkshire! Granny Fart was a gruesome character with a face that could stop a clock. She resembled the child catcher who starred in the movie *Chitty Chitty Bang Bang*. So frightening was her face, if you were unfortunate enough to stumble near her, you would shake like a dog and freeze on the spot. With her bloodcurdling laugh and menacing demeanour, she could have given Freddy Krueger (fear inspiring bogeyman from 'Nightmare on Elm Street') a run for his money.

Kicking a tin can around the street one September morning, me and the boys decided out of boredom and hunger that a visit to Granny Fart's orchard would lift morale and spirits, so off we trundled. On the way, we bumped into a classmate known as Smig who was a real character and possessed a propensity for making people laugh. He was also suffering from acute boredom so he decided to tag along. What a bunch of miscreants we looked with our snotty noses and scraggy apparel, all bound for an afternoon of thieving. As we neared the police station, the sight of Police Constable Pilsbury stopped us in our tracks.

"Where the bloody hell do you think you little shits are going today?" said the copper, exhibiting disapproval.

"We're going 'bob-a-jobbing' sir," Smig replied politely, with a hint of irony in his voice.

Now bob-a-jobbing was popular back then with the cubs and scouts, of which there were numerous packs in the area. A *bob* was a slang word meaning a shilling, which in today's currency represents five pence. You'd ask neighbours and friends if they required any odd jobs that needed carrying out, and if so, did them for a shilling per job (car cleaning, grass cutting, sweeping yards, etc). Bob-a-Job Week was carried out on a specific week every year, agreed by the local scout troops and was deemed respectable by all and sundry. In his wisdom and duplicity, Smig decided this would be seen as acceptable in the eyes of the law and credit to him, it worked. PC Pilsbury just muttered some obscenities under his breath, gave us all an evil stare, and plodded off back into the station to carry on reading his special magazines, which he carried underneath his tunic (you know, the sort of magazines that were seen to be a "hymn of praise" to the naked female form by men—especially policemen).

Feeling somewhat relieved, we marched on, but at a quicker pace, with our little "chocolate starfishes" (bottoms) still twitching. After twenty minutes or so, we arrived at our destination, faces flushed and fingers at the ready. Now, Granny's large orchard was cut off from the footpath by the beck, which was deeper and wider at this point. There was no way of jumping over or wading across it because of the depth and fast flowing water. It didn't help that a sewage pipe joined the stream at this juncture, spewing out a deluge of floating turds and effluence into the water.

The sewer pipe was wide enough across to walk on, but was virtually impassable due to having a crown of metal spikes four feet long and six inches wide, encircling each end. This metal tiara claimed many a testicle, and if it was ever breached, had to be done so gingerly (and carefully). It was, however, the only feasible way into the orchard without getting half-drowned and carried off in the current—not to mention being poisoned en route. On previous expeditions, we had tried unsuccessfully to construct our own pontoon, and on one occasion, even attempted pole vaulting with large wooden spears—but unsuccessfully. The only way, however dangerous, was over the sewer pipe.

The thought of those juicy apples would not leave us so we sat down in a circle on the bank side and collectively began to think of new ways to cross the beck. Several gormless suggestions were offered, and after much arguing and deliberation, it was decided that the sewage pipe was still the only viable option. I must point out that the same decision process took place every year, due to the fact that there was no other easy way in. So why we bothered arguing and trying different methods and routes is beyond normal comprehension, and a complete waste of everyone's time. Probably, like most men, we just liked having meetings...

Defiantly protective as it barred our way, our metal-pronged adversary stood proudly before us with its spines pointing skywards like a sunburst around the circumference of the pipe. It seemed to beckon us, eager to claim another bollock from a nervous challenger. My brother came up with a suggestion of draping our coats over the prongs, which is something we used to do when climbing over barbed wire, and did prove effective in limiting damage to our hands and legs. Smig questioned this idea because he said that if we used our coats, we wouldn't have sufficient pockets to store our booty when stealing the apples—and like the SAS, we had to be in and out as quickly as possible, laden with maximum goodies.

Time was of the essence due to Granny Fart possessing a rice gun and being a crack shot. Given the opportunity, she rarely missed her target—and if you have ever had the misfortune of being shot with rice from close quarters, I can tell you emphatically that the pain is unbearable. After a short debate, we decided to compromise and only use one coat to mask the metal spikes. We formed a chain and, taking great care with both the ascent and descent, we helped each other one by one over the first set of railings back onto the pipe. We carried out the same procedure on reaching the second set of spiny railings in order to protect our crown jewels, and fortunately, it worked. At last, we had breached the defences and were in the Garden of Eden, eagerly eyeing the big juicy fruit and dreaming of sinking our gnashers into the firm fleshy skins of the Bramleys and the fine crispy textures of the Golden Russets. The firmness and smell of an apple are good indicators of its taste and flavour. I particularly love the tartness and acidity of Bramley apples with their rock-hard skins and sour flavour, which when bitten into, cause your taste buds to explode. My memories of Granny Fart's apples are still as vivid to me now as they were then.

Checking that the coast was clear, we slowly and silently made our way up into the orchard. I enjoyed watching the rest of the gang licking their lips in anticipation of the delicious taste of the apples. Even the normally verbose Smig was as quiet as death itself. By now we were all ravenous, as hunger had really kicked in. Another check was made, all was well, and so we began our ascent into the trees. Like nimble, thieving monkeys, we were soon perched high in the trees, making one last scan of the orchard to finally ensure Granny Fart was not around.

Everything looked and seemed okay, so we started systematically stripping the trees of their fruit and stuffing the apples into our pockets. Like a plague of locusts, we were laden with our loot in seconds.

Ensconced high up in the branches, we all felt rather elated by our achievements—but alas, this was very short-lived. Through the leafy boughs of the orchard's trees a diminutive figure was spotted lurking in the background, barely visible, due to the excellent camouflage she was wearing. With a shock I discovered that Granny Fart had me in her sights, ready to blast me out of the tree. I quickly alerted the lads to the danger we were about to face by quickly and silently dropping straight down, out of the tree at the speed of sound; I've always been a team player.

BANG! An almighty booming noise ricocheted around the orchard, and the rest all descended to earth like lead. The sound was deafening, as flying rice peppered the air about us, hitting several of us on the arms and legs so much was the spread and range of the actual gunfire.

I yelled out at the top of my voice, "Chuffino-rah!" (A special Yorkshire expletive.) This was soon followed by, "Fookin' hell!"

Wow, did it hurt. Red hot rice showering the backs of my calf muscles was worse than having someone rip out my eyes and then piss in my brain. (All right, I *am* prone to the *occasional* gross exaggeration.) On a more serious note, try to imagine having thousands of needles stuck into your skin and then follow this up with molten piss and vinegar dressing being rubbed into the affected areas. To further worsen the situation, I was hit with the little brown bullets in mid air as I leapt from the tree. Granny was either a brilliant shot or just lucky that day. Due to the immense pain, I didn't concentrate on my landing and hit the floor with the grace of a rhino, winding myself in the process.

Paralysed by both pain and fear, I noticed Granny reloading her gun, ready for the second shot. Most folk would have been happy hitting the target once, but Granny had other ideas. There seemed little point in procrastinating and hanging around so I managed to pull myself up, with a Herculean struggle, and hobble off towards the stream. The rest of the gang had scattered like rats deserting a sinking ship, and in the chaos, I suddenly realised that I had lost my bearings and was heading *towards* Granny—not away from her as I had intended.

I recall thinking to myself that even a rhesus monkey or a jackass wouldn't make this mistake—so I about turned, only to hear the gun go off again. This time her target was somewhat nearer to her and stood upright, with no branches and tree trunks for protection. The rice lashed my bare legs for the second time, causing me to instantly shit myself. Yes, folks—I emptied my entire bowels in one, straight into my underwear and shorts. The smell was revolting, but it *did* allow me sufficient time to take my mind off the gunshot wounds and concentrate my thoughts and efforts on getting to the stream in order to submerge myself in its cool waters, and wash my soiled clothing.

By this time the lads had reached the sewer pipe and were frantically forcing the person in front of them over the metal spikes, so as to escape any more of Granny's shots. Now as I previously explained, getting over these perilous spiny railings needed care and skill—not to mention time, which none of them had. Pushing and shoving became the order of the day, and the lack of teamwork was very evident. Swearing, spitting, screaming, crying…

Granny, fortunately for us, had just jammed her gun, preventing her from taking a third shot. Watching Smig getting the arse of his pants ripped out and Webbo skewering his hand on one of the metal spikes made me feel a bit better about my own injuries. Craig was yelling at Webbo to hurry up, and Ginner was screeching at Craig to get a move on. It was complete pandemonium. The only thing that remained perfectly calm throughout the episode was the sewer pipe, which one by one claimed individual trophies from its unwilling victims. Blood, clothing and body parts soon decorated its spines, as once again the crafty concrete tube had wreaked its vengeance upon us to maximum effect. We were always ill-equipped to cross this battlefield and completely crazy to even attempt it, but every year, come September, we were there on the bank side being seduced by the fruits of the orchard.

Adults shooting children was acceptable back then. People also could and did defend their properties from thieves and burglars with whatever means they had at their disposal. Granny Fart happened to possess a rice gun, which when necessary, she regularly used; so we should have known better. Apple scrumping was daytime thieving, whilst house breaking was usually nocturnal. We should have swapped these two activities around in order to lessen injury and reduce the risks of getting caught.

Another little tip I will share with you is when thieving, always don a mournful, deadpan expression, as it doesn't draw attention to you. Slow everything down, then grab your loot and run like fuck.

Chapter 19

Uncle Noggin

Coming from a family of lunatics and eccentrics does have its upsides. No matter how crazy you think you are, there is always someone much more afflicted. Uncle Noggin was a magnificent example of sheer madness. I loved being in his company, because, like Uncle Tony, you never knew what was going to happen—so it made life much more interesting. Uncle Noggin was a cross between Spike Milligan, the Irish comic genius, and Rasputin, the mad Russian monk. He was well over six feet tall and as thin as a bean pole. His hair style could have started a revolution.

He was virtually bald on the top of his head, but had a considerable length of hair side (about eighteen inches), on his left side. This section of hair was carefully sculptured and used for a makeshift "comb over," which allowed him to drag the hair from the side and plaster it with oil over the top to give the effect of a full head of hair. Now let's get one thing straight—comb overs are a disaster. They look ridiculous and don't fool anyone—including blind people.

They say that if you go bald at the front of your head, you are a good thinker. If you go bald at the back of your head, you are a good lover. If you go bald all over, you *think* you are a good lover! On a positive note, the sensational footballer David Beckham has single-handedly made baldness and shaved heads acceptable to the rest of society. He has also made tattooists all over the world very grateful, and rich. When an icon of this magnitude shaves his head bald, it suddenly sends out a message to the masses: "Bald is cool." I personally would like to thank him for this.

However, having followed his example in the hair department, I do wish that I had steered well clear of having the back of my neck tattooed at the age of forty-five with *Cut Here*. It looks rather foolish when I'm serving mass. (Only joking, all you Catholics out there—I'm still not allowed back into church yet.) I know certain people think that going bald prematurely, and/or indeed gradually over a sustained period, makes them less of a man. Well, I can speak from personal experience here and tell you that this is definitely true!

They used to tell us at junior school that if you wore a hat a lot it would make you go bald. They also advised us that when we got older not to push fat women upstairs backwards as this would contribute to losing our hair by wearing it away. I ignored my teachers and did both of these things and ended up being as bald as a coot by the age of fifteen. I recently bumped into an old primary school friend who I hadn't seen for thirty-odd years. She approached me over the bacon counter and introduced herself to me. After a few minutes, I felt intrigued to ask her how she had recognised me after so many years. After all, the last time we had seen each other was when we were ten years old. She laughed out loud, and told me that I hadn't changed one jot.

"So I was bald when I was ten," I said, storming off in the direction of pickles and spices.

The one thing you have to do when going bald is to be able to laugh at yourself, because everybody else does. Being bald does have its disadvantages, like realising that you're using more soap when washing your face and scraping your skin down to the marrow,

to sustain the clean, oiled look. But hey, think on …
no head lice, no expensive visits to the barbers, no
styling gel, no grooming, no girlfriends … inferior-
ity complex, depression. Always think beyond these
boundaries and limitations and wear a wig. I do.

Getting back to Uncle Noggin's creative hair style,
his dress sense also left a lot to be desired. He always
wore grey suits purchased from local charity shops,
which were all too short—especially on his legs. This
accentuated his gangly frame and made him look
even taller than he actually was. When people wore
trousers too short in the leg, onlookers would say to
them, "What's up mate, has the cat died?"

With Noggin's dress code, *drab* and *dour* are
words that spring to mind. His brother once said that
he'd seen better dressed salads, and if Noggin kept
his clothes on long enough, they would come back
into fashion.

Noggin didn't mind the ridicule as he thought it
was all directed towards the imaginary friend who
used to float around the top of his head. This gentleman was referred to as Brother Syrenus, even though
Noggin was of no religious persuasion. Where
Brother Syrenus came from is anyone's guess, but in
Noggin's world he existed and Noggin consulted him
on everything. If you asked Uncle Noggin a question, he would raise his eyes towards the heavens to
seek spiritual guidance from Syrenus. Only after he
had debated the issue in his head with the brother
would he answer—so you can imagine how strange
and prolonged the conversations were with Noggin.
People would think him mad and they were right.
They would also lose patience with him, get bored
waiting for answers, and just walk off. I didn't mind
a hoot because I always addressed Syrenus directly
and cut out the middle man. Noggin never quibbled

with me over this, and seemed genuinely pleased that I also answered my own questions—via Syrenus, of course!

Noggin went years without being diagnosed as suffering from schizophrenia, a mental disorder which causes undue stress. People who are afflicted with this condition have problems with their thought process and tend to shun the outside world and withdraw from society in general. Schizophrenics have delusions, disordered thinking, and may exhibit unusual behavioural problems and speech malfunctions.

Unknown by most, schizophrenia is a complex illness which not only affects the patient, but also the people around them. It is a lifelong illness, and needs to be monitored and controlled with medication and professional support. The condition can cause violent outbursts, but this side of the disorder didn't affect Noggin. Being a small child, I had no idea what Noggin was suffering from so I just thought him mildly insane. He was great company, and I innocently thought it was part of his makeup. He was different and bloody funny with it.

Noggin's idiosyncrasies and mannerisms made him excellent company for me. He used to blink his eyes when he turned the lights on and off so as not to see the evil powers of electricity. He also used to make me kneel with him on the cobbled kitchen floor and pray for his false teeth to the welsh dresser. To say he was mad was an understatement. He was raving bonkers, and I loved it. He also had an imaginary dog called Bolongo, whom he would order off the sofa. Bolongo was fed dog meat and milk every night prior to Noggin retiring to bed. Each morning, the food and liquid had vanished, and no one knew where or how.

Noggin would throw a ball across the floor in the sitting-room and instruct Bolongo to retrieve it. I would piss my sides when Noggin would get up out of his threadbare armchair and bring the ball back himself. He would then proceed to shout at the dog and call it stupid for not carrying out such a simple task. This would go on for hours, and like a real life dog, Noggin never tired of playing the game. I would just sit there spellbound at Noggin's antics, occasionally pretending to pat the dog on the head and telling him to sit down beside me. On one occasion, Noggin informed me that Bolongo had bitten him and showed me the cuts to prove it. I can honestly say that his lacerated hand did look like a dog had savaged it—and considering it happened in Noggin's bedroom in the middle of the night, while I was staying, proved a little uncomfortable for me, I can tell you.

One weekend, my Mum requested that I stayed with Uncle Noggin to keep him company, due to the fact he'd been feeling rather strange. I should have disputed both these points on the grounds that he possessed more company (imaginary of course) in his head, and as for feeling strange, there was none stranger than Noggin to walk this earth!

Reluctantly, on this occasion, I went and have been regretting it ever since. Firstly, Uncle Noggin insisted on picking me up from home with his motorbike and sidecar. They were all the rage back then and thought of as being pretty cool. Noggin was a decent driver, and his vehicle was in good condition. The problem was that with the particular ride, Noggin insisted that we drive in the middle of the road to let other vehicles pass us on either side. There was no use in me valiantly trying to explain to him that this was illegal and suicidal. After listening to my suggestion and having consulted Syrenus, he just looked at me as if I was stupid, tutted, and clipped me around the back of my head. With brute force he bungled me in the side compartment like a kidnap victim, and off we went. The noise from the motorcycle was extremely loud, but I could just about make out what Noggin was suggesting to me through the glass cockpit.

"We're going to play a little game I've just invented with Brother Syrenus. I'm going to see how far I can drive with my eyes shut and for how long," he said.

What the fuck was the lunatic thinking?

He didn't comprehend my terrified expression and ignored my nob-head hand signals. He just closed his eyes and burst into hysterical laughter. Within three seconds we'd clipped the side of the kerb, and the sidecar became detached from the motorbike with me holed up inside it. I was now spiralling down the road in my metal and glass shell with no means of steering or control. After what seemed like an eternity, I came to an abrupt halt when the wheel dislodged itself from the undercarriage and propelled me straight through the hawthorn hedge of Mr Hoskin's garden. Luckily for me, the hedge acted like a buffer and slowed my rocket down.

I scrambled out of the compartment, shaken and stirred, only to see Noggin heading directly towards the front door of the local vicar's house. By now, Noggin had left the road and careered up the driveway of the vicarage. Unbelievably, his eyes were still firmly closed, and I still could hear him laughing and talking to who I guessed was still Syrenus. Just as I was about to shout a warning to alert Noggin to the impending danger, the vicar happened to open the door. Noggin's motorcycle smashed into the steps leading up to the vicar's front doorway, launching Noggin off the saddle and into the vicarage vestibule. Miraculously, Noggin was unhurt. The vicar, however, broke four ribs and lost six teeth. Throughout this entire calamitous stunt, Noggin's eyes remained tightly shut. When the now toothless vicar managed to clamber back up to his feet, he looked at Noggin in complete bewilderment.

Before he could say anything to him, Noggin opened his eyes and said, "Amen."

We hobbled the rest of the way home, leaving the vicar semi-conscious and dazed. It was no use discussing our little suicide mission as Noggin was off with the fairies, thinking up other ruses to entertain me for the latter part of the evening. When we finally arrived home, Noggin placed Bolongo's supper near the kitchen door and informed me that Syrenus was suffering from fatigue and retiring to the monastery. He went on to add that a new friend called Wilfred had recently come into his life, and he wanted to stay up into the wee small hours and play. After what I'd just been put through, you would think me barmy to take up his offer and stay in the house with him. But it was late by now, and I was intrigued to meet Wilfred.

Within minutes, Wilfred was on the scene—via the thoughts and mind of Noggin. I soon discovered that Wilfred was in fact a child of about ten and very naughty.

It is amazing and disturbing to see a person change personalities so rapidly and take on all new traits and different speech patterns. At the last count before Noggin passed away, he was dealing with six personalities—all completely different and all floating above his head in his imaginary world. The medical profession is still at odds with the idea of split personalities, and some highly regarded doctors still dismiss it entirely. This illness affects approximately 2% of the population and occurs equally between men and women. Factors contributing to the illness can be stress, social isolation, trauma, injury to the brain, and drug dependency, but no specific factor has been identified as the single cause.

When I was observing Noggin from a safe distance, the look on his face as he was waiting for answers to his questions and guidance from his hallucinatory friends, was heartbreaking. He would ask them a question out loud and then patiently stare upwards into space, waiting for the response. When the answer came back, he would lower his gaze to meet yours and reply using whichever personality was communicating through him at the time. Sometimes he would pose a problem to Wilfred, but Freda would answer it. He never knew, and neither did you.

In one of his rare, nearly lucid, moments, he turned to me and said, "I used to be schizophrenic, but I'm all right now. No you're not. Yes I am. No you're not."

The poor man had no chance, but at least he was blessed with company and was never lonely. Watching him play cards with himself was fun, if not a little frightening. Accusing yourself of cheating seems barmy, and arguing about playing the wrong card with people who exist only in your world must be frustrating, to say the least. Always looking skywards, waiting for answers and assistance, Noggin went through life oblivious to the real world—ignorant of its problems and wars, and blissfully unaware of its dangers.

I remember once visiting Noggin when he was carrying out a bit of joinery work in his kitchen. He was knocking a nail into the wall when he said, "Oh fuck, that fucker's fucked. Fuck off and fetch another fucker."

The trouble with this is that I knew exactly what he meant!

Noggin's episodes did get progressively worse as he got older. Sometimes he appeared just distant and vague. Other times he actually became one of his alter egos and took on all their traits and characteristics. You could tell when he was changing character by the dramatic facial changes. These were quickly followed by a change in the pitch of his vocal range, depending on which person he had morphed into.

When Wilfred came onto the scene that night, Noggin altered nearly beyond recognition. This little imp was trouble, but in the nicest possible way. Wilfred's enunciation was completely different from that of Noggin's, and somewhat brusque. Wilfred was a frolicsome and sprightly young lad, full of energy. He immediately started making spurious remarks about Syrenus, who of course thought himself infallible. Wilfred kept banging on about how Syrenus was full of shit, and it was at this stage I realised Wilfred was not addressing me—he was talking directly to Noggin, who happened to be trapped inside his own head. Wilfred was totally oblivious to me, and I posed no threat to him or indeed to any of the other personalities whatsoever. I was merely the audience, being entertained for free!

It was fascinating to witness such transformations taking place right in front of my eyes in Noggin. It was like watching a surreal play acted out with the skill to rival the renowned actor Sir Alec Guinness, in the 1950 Ealing comedy *Kind Hearts and Coronets* in which he played eight different roles. Noggin, however, hadn't had any acting lessons and didn't change costumes—only personalities.

Witnessing the interplay between each character and the banter coming from Uncle Noggin at such a breakneck pace was breathtaking, and wildly amusing. Syrenus called Wilfred a "reprobate and evildoer" and said that he should be soundly thrashed. Wilfred responded by saying that Syrenus was a pain in the apse! The conversation came to a swift end when Noggin reappeared and called the pair of them "vociferous buggers".

Uncle Noggin degenerated rapidly following my visit—such was the cruelness of his illness. He kept forgetting to take his medication, and when he did take it, he often took too much, which turned him into a zombie or a madman. There seemed to be no in between. He was taken to live with his aging mother. On one particular occasion, he was arguing with his mother over whether to have beans or peas for dinner. He wanted beans, and she wanted peas. To settle the quarrel, Noggin bashed his mother over the head with a metal poker (which seemed somewhat excessive to me), splitting her cranium in two. The moral of this story is -choose beans every time!

The last time I saw Noggin, he was much happier and relaxed. I could hear him screaming and howling with laughter in the front room of his house. When I asked his mother what he was chortling at, she informed me that he was watching his favourite television programme. I was curious to see what this programme was, only to find that he was staring at the Test Card. *Test Card F*, as it was known, created by the BBC and first broadcast in 1967 on BBC2. It was a static image of a young girl playing noughts and crosses, with a clown doll. This test card was shown when the transmitter was active, but no programme was being broadcast. It was often aired during down-time on BBC1. No sound and a still image is enough to drive anyone insane. But Noggin already liked this particular game, so he carried on staring at the same image for hours, laughing hysterically.

My visits to Uncle Noggin's were ephemeral and too infrequent. I still miss his bizarre behaviour and his exploits. One of his last personalities to appear was a Polish immigrant called Roman. My Mum took Noggin to the opticians when he was under the spell of Roman. The optician showed him a card with the letters C Z W I X N O S T A C Z.

"Can you read that?" he said.

Noggin (or Roman, the Polish immigrant) answered, "Read it? I fucking know the bloke!"

Noggin was a gentleman who was diagnosed too late in his life with this terrible illness, so any chance of real help was gone. His family just let him get on with it, as he was too much of a burden for them. I never once felt at risk in his company other than the episode on the motorbike, and always found him entertaining. Children today would never be allowed to mix and stay with people in this condition. But I was, and I'm eternally grateful.

They say that the line between genius and madness is a very fine one. I often wonder which side of the line I'm on…

Chapter 20

Ferreting with Obadiah

A classmate of mine kindly offered to sell me a ferret, as his albino had recently given birth. Now a ferret is like a bigger version of a stoat. They can live for up to ten years (average life expectancy is four to five years) and grow to twenty-four inches long. Albino ferrets are sometimes considered second-class when compared to the coloured varieties, but if you hunt with an albino, they are much easier to spot. Male ferrets, or "hobs" as they are known, tend to grow much larger than females or "jills", as they are often referred to. Ferrets can make excellent pets, but do need proper care and attention. I once heard my Grandad saying that ferrets were just half tame polecats, and neither use nor ornament to man or beast—I guess he didn't like them. I was overjoyed at the prospect of owning my own ferret, and even happier when my pal Potter, who was selling the animal, decided he would rather have a Kestrel's egg instead of the cash. *Fair swap* I thought, and the deal was done.

If you came from Northern England in the '60s, the idea of keeping a pet for pleasure was frowned upon. Pets were usually dogs or pigeons, and most of these had to earn their keep by either guarding properties or winning races. People who kept ferrets had them for one reason and one reason only: to help catch rabbits. Ferrets were working animals and very effective in flushing out a rabbit warren of its inhabit-ants. Hunting with ferrets or ferreting, as it is more commonly known, dates back thousands of years to ancient Greece.

Up to and including the Second World War, ferreting was a very common sport, especially with Northern English folk. In the early 1950s, ferreting spiralled into decline when farmers and landowners deliberately introduced *myxomatosis* into the countryside—a disease which infects rabbits. By the mid 1950s, almost 95% of the rabbit population of the UK was wiped out. The disease is caused by the myxoma virus and is spread by fleas and mosquitoes. If you ever have the misfortune to see a rabbit suffering from this dreadful condition, I can honestly say that it is heartbreaking. Their eyes puff out and they go blind and lethargic, unable to move easily. It's a horrendous sight. I recently saw a rabbit suffering from myxomatosis in a nearby village, so I'm sorry to report that the disease is still with us to this day.

One Saturday morning, Potter arrived at our house and presented me with my new pet. I named him Obadiah, after my aunt. In preparation, I'd built a hutch and pen for him behind the coalhouse. I couldn't wait to bed him in and get to know him. When a ferret is not in work mode, it requires to be handled regularly, and its health and welfare need managing correctly. They want to be stimulated and kept active with toys and disused pipes for them to run through. Their diet is also vitally important, which should include dry mix as well as fresh meat. Like a complete arsehole, I used to feed Obadiah all kinds of rubbish and now realise that this was entirely wrong and inappropriate—chewing gum and currants are certainly not to be recommended.

After a few months, I decided that it was time to take my ferret out hunting, and Potter agreed to show me the ropes. We set off for Hooton Levitt at first light, as Potter was familiar with a couple of warrens there. Along with our ferreting equipment, we took our dogs Kesh and Sam with us. Our equipment comprised of catapults, ammo, a spade, purse nets, hessian sacks to keep the ferrets in, and a skinning knife, which had to be sheathed as it was so sharp. Whenever I carried my catapult with me, I always draped it around my neck and inside my jumper for concealment. Potter, however, had a quite different approach to hiding his weapon, as he inverted his catapult and stuffed it down his underpants so it rested on his prick, with the handle pointed upwards. He told me that his father had taught him to do this, on the chance that if a gamekeeper or policeman caught and searched you, the last place that they would look would be down your pants—and to the casual observer, you gave the impression of being permanently aroused.

When going out ferreting, it's always a good idea to get the landowner's permission. Back then, we never bothered and just trespassed wherever and whenever we liked. We also never put our dogs on leashes, as the dogs were well trained. Well this is not exactly true. My dog, Kesh, was very obedient and would walk to heel, he would also respond to commands and stay at my side; the only time this rule was flagrantly ignored was when a cat, rabbit, or indeed any other furry creature ventured into his domain. Then it was "head down, arse up", and off he went, sometimes for days on end.

Throughout the entire journey, Potter kept rabbiting on (sorry) about how good his ferret was. He had bought it from good working stock and paid a lot of money for it. (Now ferrets are, and were, as cheap as chips, so why he'd paid a shed-load of cash for it I had no idea.) He rambled on and on about how many rabbits it had flushed out and how it was far and above superior to any other ferret he had come across. I for one can't stand a show-off, and Potter could have won a gold medal for boasting that morning. The bullshit he was spouting about his prize animal was relentless. He just wouldn't button it.

After arriving at our destination, we quickly found an active warren and proceeded to net it up. This is done by identifying the main entrance into the burrow. A purse net is then placed inside the mouth of the hole, ensuring that the spread of the net covers the entire aperture of the hole. A peg is attached to the net and then firmly staked into the ground above the hole to secure the net in place. The purse net is equipped with a drawstring around its circumference, so when the intended prey runs into the mesh, it pulls the net tight shut and closes on it on impact, thus trapping the rabbit. All other remaining bolt-holes and pop-up holes are identified and netted accordingly. After that, it's a case of lifting up the entry net to the main hole and popping in the ferret, which then travels through the burrows, flushing the rabbits out into the waiting nets.

With dogs on standby and everything in place, Potter slowly and carefully opened his sack, ready to release the ferret. Unfortunately, at the very instant his animal peaked out of the sack into the sunlight, my dog leapt up and bit Potter's ferret's head clean off. (The SAS would have been proud of how expertly and cleanly my dog took out this particular ferret.) Potter was distraught and burst into floods of tears. I tried in vain to retrieve the poor ferret's head, but Kesh had swallowed it whole. I don't know what I would have done if I'd have recovered the head—

probably tried to stick it back on. (Dogs 1, Ferrets 0.)

When hunting with ferrets, it is recommended to put at least two of them down the hole. We hadn't even managed to get one of the dear creatures fully out of the sack before it had been assassinated by my bloody hound. Potter was still speechless, so to try and ease the situation, I suggested that we should give Obadiah a chance, as everything was set up. He mumbled something to me, which sounded like "thick cut," and I proceeded to introduce my ferret into the main entrance of the burrow. Within seconds, Obadiah was gone, descending into the bowels of the earth in search of fresh juicy meat. I checked again to ensure all remaining pop-up holes were netted and loaded my catapult for backup in case any managed to escape from a hole we hadn't detected. Potter assured me that the burrow was occupied and told me to ready the dogs as a further back-up. My heart was pounding, and I could sense something was about to happen at any second. It did.

I was aiming my catapult in the general direction of the warren, elastic straining to breaking point, pouch loaded with a ball bearing, when suddenly I felt a lash across my left hand. Potter screamed out in pain—so much that it startled my dog to the extent that it jumped up at him and proceeded to sink its teeth into his leg. I quickly removed the dog from Potter by doing what all dog handlers suggest: I kicked it straight in its knackers. Hey, presto, it worked. The dog yelped in pain, released Potter, and made off to the nearby woods with Potter's dog in hot pursuit.

I realised something was wrong while looking at my mate, who was now bent double, holding his face with one hand and his leg with the other, blood everywhere, and still crying loudly. Several minutes had passed, and through sobbing words punctuated with deep panting noises, I began to understand what had happened. I had inadvertently, and don't ask me why, fired the catapult, propelling the ball bearing like a speeding bullet into the ground. By a stroke of unbelievably bad luck, the spherical missile had hit a half submerged rock, causing it to ricochet in the direction of Potter. Fortunately it only hit him on the tip of his nose, hence the fountain of blood. We used the empty sack to stem the bleeding, and I suggested that he just sit down for a while well out of the way. I apologised profusely for my actions and comforted him by telling him he could have lost his eye—but to no avail. He went home alone, ferretless, clutching a bloodied sack and heavy heart. Still feeling completely shit about what I'd done to Potter, I suddenly remembered that my ferret was still down the hole.

I have been ferreting on many occasions and come home empty-handed. This happens when the burrow is unoccupied or you've missed netting a pop-up hole, or as it happens in most cases, when the ferret kills underground. Hobs or male ferrets are more likely to do this, and when they've feasted on the rabbit, they will "lay-up" and sleep next to the kill. If this occurs, the only way to retrieve your ferret is by digging it out with a spade. This can take ages and is back-breaking work. When digging out, it does help if you have another ferret, preferably a hob, which has a line attached to it. When the hob is introduced, it seeks out the ferret which has lain-up and scares it out of the burrow. It then takes its place at the kill site. Because this ferret has a draw line attached to it, locating it is a lot easier. It is then a case of excavating the soil until you reach the second hob.

After waiting twenty minutes, it slowly dawned on me that my ferret had killed underground and was laying-up. With no other ferret, no dogs, no mate, and no spade (Potter's spade, so he'd taken it back home with him), I was up shit creek without a paddle. Knowing this, most kids would have given up and called it a day. Not me. I was determined to go home with Obadiah if it killed me. I've never been blessed with good luck, and over the years, when I land myself in situations similar to this one, I just accept it and carry on.

Digging out your ferret without a spade is difficult enough. Not having a bleeding clue where the damn thing is also doesn't help matters. With a deep sigh, I pondered what to do next. Miraculously (even God must have felt sorry for me that day), hidden in the gorse bush nearby was a spade that some other ferreters had left from a previous hunt. My spirits were lifted, and I immediately plunged the spade into the soil around the entrance hole. A loud *snap* suddenly resonated around me. The wooden shaft had snapped in half, due to it being left out in the elements too long. It is at this point of the operation that I began to cry in desperation. What more could go wrong?

By chance, a farmer happened to be passing by, and hearing my cries, stopped to assess the situation.

"What's wrong, young feller me lad?" he said.

"I've lost the will to live," I replied. I explained my predicament, and the farmer listened patiently, empathising with my dilemma. It never once entered my head that I was trespassing on his land.

"Is this your dog?" he said, dragging Kesh from behind him on a piece of rope.

I explained what had happened and told him the truth, as there seemed no point in lying. He was very understanding and handed me the dog back, saying that he would keep the pheasant that Kesh had recently killed. Regarding the ferret, he said he would go and get his shovel and help me to retrieve him, which I thought was extremely kind. It was at this precise moment that Obadiah appeared at the entrance of the warren. Sated and content, he sauntered towards me, oblivious to the situation. I gently picked him up and placed him back in his carrying sack. The farmer then patted me on the head, swiftly kicked me up the arse, and bid me farewell.

The entire hunt had been a disaster, so I decided to wing my way home and forget it ever happened. As I lunged forward from the force of the farmer's size eleven shoes, he called for me to halt. He reached into the bag he was carrying, which happened to be full of dead rabbits.

"Here you are you little bugger. Take this home to your Mum and ask her to prepare and cook it. You bloody well know you shouldn't be here, and if I catch you again, I'll skin you alive."

Not wanting to look a gift horse in the mouth, I thanked him and ran all the way home. When I arrived back, my Mum was as pleased as punch that I had caught a rabbit. I didn't tell her the full story for obvious reasons. Mum previously worked part-time in a butcher's shop so when it came to paunching—removing the guts, etc.—I left it to her. She was an expert when it came to the art of skinning and paunching.

Later I did go on a successful hunt with Potter, who showed me the technique of "thumbing and legging". When you caught a rabbit in a purse net, the first thing you had to do was "neck it" by hitting it hard on the back of the neck to kill it instantly. Once the rabbit was dead you held it upside down, gripped its hind leg, and pressed inwards and downwards with your thumb to relieve the rabbit of excess urine. The hind leg was then slit using your sharp skinning knife, and the remaining hind leg was shoved through the slit. The heel of this leg was nicked to secure it and a walking stick or pole was inserted through the slit in order to carry the dead rabbit.

I used to see grown men proudly marching through the village with six or seven rabbits dangling from their poles. The meat was fresh, organic, and tasted beautiful. It's a pity that it is not eaten more often now, as the flavour and taste is superb. Another fine meal we occasionally had back then as a treat was jugged hare, which tasted wonderful and also made a fabulous wig!

I miss ferreting, but I don't miss seeing rabbits killed. I've become a softie when it comes to rabbits due to the fact that my children kept them as pets, and over time, I grew to like them. When I was growing up, the thought of keeping a rabbit as a pet was preposterous. Rabbits were for the pot—it was as simple as that.

To end this chapter, I'd like to share with you an interesting fact regarding ferrets. I recently read this in my one of my son's pornographic magazines, purporting to be a "lad's mag". Under the section called "Arses and Tits in yer Face," it said that a weird but true fact was that the collective noun for a group of ferrets was a "business". Now I hope you will all sleep better knowing that!

Chapter 21
Camping Out

Sleeping under canvas is a magnificent experience and one I would highly recommend. The smell of the tarpaulin and stale urine conjures up wonderful memories. I camped out with my cub scout pack on numerous occasions, which was fun—but this was nothing compared with the enjoyment I had when camping out with my mates in their back gardens.

Perhaps the idea of camping out in an overgrown garden in a mining village doesn't quite grab you by the balls and set the imagination running wild, but for me it was sheer bliss. I couldn't have been happier if I'd slept under the stars at Uluru in Australia with the aborigines. The proximity from the actual camp-site to the house was no more than ten feet, but it might well have been a million miles for all I cared. Once we pitched our tent and night had fallen, we were transported to a different world—a world of axe murderers and practical jokes.

Our neighbour, Spuggie (a word we used for sparrows), had a two-man Vango tent that his elder brother had "borrowed" from his scout pack. Vango tents are still popular today, and exceptionally good quality. The only problem we encountered with the actual two-man shelter was that six of us camped out in it! This wouldn't have been such a big deal with me, but Spuggie's brother, Ron, would always insist on spending the night with us. He was a churlish lad who needed another chip on his other shoulder to balance him out. Being several years older than the rest of us naturally gave him the role of leader and bully boy. He told us that what he'd forgotten about camping we would never know. (Take a moment to think about how ridiculous that sounds.) Another one of his sayings went along the lines of, "He who laughs first laughs last," and my favourite one was, "The problem with your lot is that you are iggorant." (Spelt the way he said it.)

Ron was a legend in his own mind, and took it upon himself to impinge on our territory and ill-treat us at every opportunity. This fourteen-year-old boy was certainly destined for university, then world leadership. He really got under my skin, and I planned numerous ways of killing him in his sleep. At times I felt compelled to use my trusty dagger on him and whittle him into a tent peg. He also smoked a lot— not because he thought he looked cool, but because he said it helped him breathe more easily. He smoked so much that when he coughed, he had a soot fall.

I saw him recently on his brand new mobility scooter in the local supermarket. He told me he was planning to go into an all inclusive old folk's home. (The only slight problem I could foresee with his plan was the small fact of him only being fifty-two years old and the home being situated in Maltby, not Benidorm!) Ron, unfortunately, had an accident at work when he was in his forties and subsequently received a huge amount of compensation, which he blew quicker than Viv Nicholson, the pools winner. He was once described as the cream of the village … rich and thick!

What made life bearable with Ron was Spuggie, who was a tenacious and gregarious young boy. He put the "F" in fun and caused me to piss my pants with laughter at his antics. He was naturally funny without ever knowing it. He was once talking to the local priest about how his Mum and Dad enjoyed camping. He went on to say how his father loved to unzip the old bag and get his pole right up. On one occasion he referred to a bell tent, which is a cone-shaped tent having a single central supporting pole, as a "bell-end" tent (bell-end—schoolboy reference to the male appendage). This wouldn't normally have been too bad, but Spuggie was on the stage speaking to the entire assembly at school at the time, telling them of his latest camping adventure with the cub scouts. He finished his little speech by saying how nice it was to sleep under a large bell-end. He said it pricked him into feeling closer to nature.

Both my brother and I loved Spuggie's company. He was easily wound up, and if pointed in the right direction, could cause chaos in an instant. He was, however, a good solid mate and never crossed either me or Craig in all the time we knew him. He could take a joke if it was from one of the gang—but if he didn't know you and thought you were taking the piss out of him, then there would be trouble afoot. I used to tell Spuggie on a regular basis that I would never take the piss out of him. After all, I went on to add, you couldn't take the piss out of shit. He always seemed satisfied with my explanation and never once questioned my superior intellect.

Spuggie was also a lad who loved a challenge and was always up for it. We once found a wasp's nest in bushes beside the rear of the tent one summer morning. We dared Spuggie to poke the nest with a stick that had a paraffin-soaked rag tied to the end of it, which was duly set alight. Spuggie proceeded to torch the entrance of the nest, and within seconds, we were being repeatedly stung by hundreds of the little bleeders. I remember shouting the word "bastards" several times aloud and frantically waving my arms about like a demented lunatic, trying to fend off the aerial onslaught and stop the incessant pain. Spuggie's dad raced down from his adjoining allotment and smacked his son straight across the face, sending his glasses flying over into the neighbouring garden. With wasps swarming all around and still stinging the shit out of us, Spuggie's dad seemed oblivious of our dilemma (and his own for that matter) and said, "I've never heard such vile and filthy language in my life. I could hear your 'bastards' from five hundred yards. Now button it and bugger off, or I'll thrash the lot of you!"

In all the pandemonium and panic, I was now sporting a wasp beard. Spuggie's father calmly walked away from the morning's festivities without a scratch, or indeed, a single sting. I ended up looking like the Elephant Man and couldn't sit down for a week. Whilst we are on the subject of wasps, I would like to share a secret with you all.

Now I know I've burdened you with my lack of good luck and I think you will sympathise, if not empathise, with my ongoing misfortunate, but on the flip side once I actually found a four-leaf clover in Byford's field in Maltby. (As you may have heard, a four-leaf clover is extremely rare and meant to bring you good luck.) I stumbled on this little gem by complete accident, and before I plucked it from the ground, I counted the individual leaves several times just to make sure. With my heart pounding like a drum and fingers twitching like a pickpocket, I quickly uprooted the plant with the hope that my bad luck was going to be a thing of the past and life was about to change for the better. Some bloody chance. As I plucked the green godsend from the earth, I inadvertently scooped up a wasp, which immediately began to sting me with the venom of a viper. Shocked and startled, I dropped the clover and concentrated all my efforts on the wasp. With my fingers throbbing, and choking back tears, I raced home in pain, not giving the four-leaf clover another thought.

Spuggie's back garden was massive compared with ours, and his father took great pride in its appearance. Back then, people either grew vegetables in their rear garden or just left it to nature and allowed theirs and other people's kids to use it as a playground. The garden at Spuggie's was totally different—manicured lawns with beautiful assortments of shrubs and plants complemented with ornamental bushes and established trees. Spuggie's dad worked for the parks department of the local Council and tended to "relocate" certain greenery as and when it became available, which was usually in the dead of night. Even though he was fanatical about his prized garden, he would allow us to set up camp on a section near the main house, which was well away from his beloved greenhouse. However, he made this magnanimous gesture only if we agreed to cut his lawns for the next fortnight.

Deal done, we excitedly began to pitch the Vango tent, all merrily whistling and singing—the anticipation of the night's ghost stories and penis competitions gripped us like a vice. Something as simple as camping out on our mate's back garden filled us all with happiness beyond compare.

It's tragic that nowadays English kids are constantly bored and seem permanently stressed out and sad. They are all so American and have lost the art of playing and having fun. My twelve-year-old boy surprised me the other day by asking me if he could camp out at his mate's house for the night. I was delighted and agreed on the spot. On the evening of the stay over, I was patiently waiting for him in the car in order to transport him up to his mate's home. After sitting alone for twenty minutes on the drive, I decided to pip the horn loudly and attract his attention from inside the house and discover what was holding him up. Much to our neighbours' annoyance, I carried on tooting the car horn, trying desperately to hurry him along.

Eventually he emerged and promptly told me to "Chill out, Grandad."

Behind him came his mother, laden down with three large bags, which she struggled to fit into the boot of the car. When I asked him what all the gear comprised of, he proceeded to advise me that he had only brought along the bare essentials for the night. I was aware that I take less luggage to Portugal with me when we go for our family summer holiday! He went on to inform me that he would have to make do with his Hugo Boss body spray, as he didn't want to appear too flash to the other guys. Bloody Hugo bloody Boss deodorant for camping! The whole idea about being away from your parents for a night is that you didn't have to wash, never mind use a body spray.

When we arrived at the house, the father kindly helped me with the mountain of gear and asked if I'd like to inspect the tent. I graciously accepted, only to be shocked to see that the tent was in fact a fourteen-foot trampoline with a purpose-made cover masquerading as a tent. When I ascended the fold-down steps into the canvas palace, which had the opulence of an Arabian tent complete with Bombay Boudoir, I was confronted with beds, wall lights, pillows, portable televisions, PSPs, iPods, mobile phones, and a laptop. I've slept in hotels that couldn't boast this kind of technology and luxury. When I asked where the campfire was going to be sited and what grub they were going to rustle up, I was looked at like some kind of freak. No fire food for these tough boys—they were having a delivery of pizza, Indian and Chinese food. The final straw was when one of the kids requested a skinny cappuccino … then I knew it was time for me to leave.

When we were camping on Spuggie's garden, all we had was each other. The entertainment was occasionally embellished with a torch or flashlight. In the pitch darkness of the interior of the tent, we would take it in turns to place the glass of the torch directly underneath our chins and flick the switch on to light up our faces. To add further amusement, we would contort our faces to resemble the old actor, Charles Laughton, who was blessed with the face of a horse's arse! Spuggie had an advantage over all of us when carrying out this mimicry, as he had a face that looked like that of a wide-mouthed frog. No matter how many times we pulled the same faces, it still made us all laugh out loud. Another game we played on each other was "fill the orifice". This game consisted of secretly choosing a victim, preferably someone who hadn't played the game before and smaller and younger than the rest of us. When the said innocent was asleep, the nominated "plugger" would whip out a tube of toothpaste and steadily fill up a hole or crack on that person. It could be his nostrils, ears, or bellybutton—whatever.

On one particular night, our intended prey was Spuggie, who had fallen into a deep sleep. I was elected plugger and decided that I would fill up Spuggie's nostrils—this I did in record time, without a movement or twitch from young Spuggie. We stared at him for a while with our torches, hoping he would wake up with stinging nasal cavities—but this proved not to be the case. I then proceeded to fill his ears, arm-pits, belly-button, toes, and finally, his arse crack. Still absolutely nothing from Spuggie—he didn't flinch at all. His brother, Ron, decided in his wisdom that Spuggie must be dead. Being on top of the situation, I carefully placed a mirror just in front of his lips to see if his breath would smear the surface of the mirror. Bingo. It worked; he was obviously still alive. We eventually got bored just waiting for Spuggie to react, and one by one, all dropped off to sleep in our sleeping bags.

Next morning, I was the first to surface and quickly and quietly woke all other gang members with the exception of Spuggie. Ron was somewhat irate with the situation he had allowed his brother to be put through and thoughtfully smacked Spuggie across the back of the head and ordered him to get up. Spuggie slowly opened his eyes in a somnolent state and yawned, which terrified the rest of us. He contorted his face a little, picked his nose, and laid back down again to return to his slumber. This really pissed off Ron, who by now was blood red in the face and starting to get his dander up.

"What's wrong with you, shit for brains?"

"Nothing Ron, I'm just knackered," was Spuggie's reply.

By now, our eyes had become accustomed to the daylight, streaming through the tent door flaps. It was then that I noticed white marks all over the inside of the tent, from one end to the other. When I went outside our canvas shelter, I also noticed the same marks all over the exterior. These white deposits were toothpaste—Spuggie's toothpaste, at that! He had obviously been sleepwalking in the night. When we told him about our fiendish trick, Spuggie leapt out of his sleeping bag and appeared to the assembled group, stark naked. He then went on to share the dream (or nightmare) that he had experienced, in which he thought he had eaten a bucket full of sour crab apples, resulting in a serious case of the shits. He vaguely remembered his arse being somewhat on fire and said the smell was so strange it made his nose burn and his eyes smart. During the night, there had been a slight downpour so in his dreamlike state, he had decided to cool his rectum on the external tent fabric. He couldn't recall how he'd divested himself of his clothes, but that was the least of his worries. By this time, we were all excitedly following his dream, second by second. (You just couldn't make this stuff up.)

Spuggie then focused his eyes directly at Ron, and asked, "Why have you got toothpaste on the end of your nose?"

Ron's face went from puce to ashen in an instant, and Spuggie came to within an inch of losing his life. We were all sworn to secrecy there and then, with the fear of death hanging over each and every one of us if we ever mentioned what had actually taken place.

When I think back to the toothpaste episode, I am reminded of a similar situation I witnessed when I was in my thirties. The company I was working for at the time had decided in its infinite wisdom that all key personnel would undertake a gruelling Outward Bound course for team-building and morale.

Total bag of shit, I thought. And surprise, surprise, I was proved right!

We spent several November nights under canvas in Banbury carrying out mindless tasks and shattering any confidence some of the quieter members of the team had. It was a joke from start to finish and cost the company a bloody fortune for nothing. People came away from the course delusional, distraught, and all in agreement about what they had achieved by attending such a course. The consensus of opinion was a resounding "Fuck all!" It was poorly organised, ill-thought out, and hadn't factored into the programme people's ages, abilities, and disabilities.

The only one decent memory of this disastrous waste of time happened on the final night. When you have slept outdoors for three days and not washed properly or eaten sufficiently, you begin to lose the will to live. Added to this fact, we were expected to build bridges with oversized plastic bottles and sisal rope, and abseil down six foot walls—you can see it was hardly SAS material. When the final task had been completed, we all decided to shit, shave, and shower, then rendezvous down at the local boozer. The instructors couldn't understand why we didn't want to all stay in our filthy apparel and have a debrief session with them over a nice cup of tea. Ignoring the pleas from our tutors, we all got absolutely wankered drunk.

The last night was spent indoors in a makeshift youth hostel. I was bunking up with a bloke who liked a drink or three, and between us, we finally managed to crash into our beds at three in the morning. In my drunken state, I took it on myself to open all the windows in the dormitory, and then proceeded to throw all my bed linen and pillows into the freezing night—well, we've all been stupidly hammered at some time or another. My roommate didn't object to my antics in the slightest, which on reflection was very reasonable of him. I then stripped myself of my remaining clothes and flaked out on the bare mattress. Within seconds I was in a complete state of comatose and frozen solid. At around five that morning, I was woken up by my bunk buddy sitting bolt upright in bed and throwing up in between his legs. He then leaned over the side of the bed and carried on removing the contents of his stomach. After what seemed like an eternity, he resumed the seated position in bed, and with his head flopped forwards into his lap, fell back into a deep sleep.

Seven that same morning, we were woken by our team leader and told to meet downstairs for breakfast at half-past. When I glanced over at my comrade, I noticed that he still had his head in between his thighs. I prodded him with my foot, and eventually he came round. Looking out into the room by the side of his bed, I watched him analyze the current situation he now found himself in.

He uttered the words, "Oh dear ... Oh very dear! What have I done?"

I then noticed that he had vomited directly into his rucksack, all over his only clean clothes. There wasn't a single speck of puke on the floor. The bed, however, was a different kettle of fish. He had chucked his guts up on top of the bed covers between his legs. Due to the fact that his head had been between his legs, he had unfortunately dunked his hair into the technicolour mess for added effect. Because I'd left open the windows, and the sub-zero temperature, his hair was now covered in a perfectly solid deep pan pizza of barf. This edible hat would have won a prize at Royal Ascot for total originality. I didn't help matters by me laughing my tits off for the next hour.

Several hours on from the pizza debacle and following a good shower and breakfast, we were all requested to meet in the conference room and share our experiences with the group leaders and rest of the party. When Mr 'Pizza Turban' stood up to make his speech on his experiences during the four-day ordeal, he started to sweat profusely. His hangover from the previous night's drinking session was starting to kick in. He began to appear flushed of face and started blowing his cheeks out a lot. Just as he was about to close his dialogue, a rogue piece of carrot appeared from behind his ear and trickled slowly down his face—he obviously hadn't washed all the vegetables out of his mop. Once again, I came to his rescue by alerting the entire group to his unfortunate dilemma and highlighting the carrot with a large pointy visual aid. I've always prided myself in being fair and helpful—and keeping everyone involved in what's happening.

I know I have digressed somewhat, but I felt I needed to share that little story with you. Getting back to camping, I can only stress how fantastic sleeping out with your mates under canvas is. Comradeship, friendship, sharing farting prowess, showing off ... the list is endless. If someone asks you to go camping, do it!

To finish this specific chapter, I will give you all several pieces of advice, which will impress your friends if you decide to go camping. If you take matches with you to start a fire, dunk the tips in nail varnish in case they get wet. If you do this, they will stay dry, and will still strike. Always wear long sleeves so you can wipe your nose. When walking past guy-ropes, always wear shoes so your toes don't get caught in them—*very* painful and can bring the tent down in one. And lastly, always have a good joke to share with your fellow campers. My favourite oldie and goldie is the following:

Sherlock Holmes and Doctor Watson go camping and pitch their tent under the stars. During the night,

Holmes wakes his trusty companion and says, "Watson, look up at the stars, and tell me what you can deduce."

Watson stares at the stars and says, "I can see millions of stars, and even if a few of those are planets, it's quite likely there are some planets like Earth. And if there are a few planets like Earth out there, there might also be life."

Holmes waits a while and replies, "Watson you idiot. Someone has stolen the tent."

Chapter 22

Sports Day and All That

Sports Day could either be a triumph for the school or a personal disaster for an individual competitor. When you fail, it can be something which affects your confidence and stays with you for the rest of your life. Brought up in conversation in later years, it can smash your self-esteem into the ground. Representing your school in a tournament, with all your parents and grandparents watching from the sidelines and willing you on to achieve your full potential and win, can be so onerous when placed on a young person's shoulders.

As I had no intention of being involved in the games in the first place, having to compete in the sack race was a real pisser—mainly due to my total lack of ability and skill. It was a real kick in the scrotum, and when ordered to do so by my inconsiderate teacher, I felt suicidal. No amount of cognitive behavioural therapy can help a child overcome a childhood sporting trauma. Carl Rogers (1902-1987), an eminent humanistic psychotherapist, developed a client-centred therapy. He claimed there were three core conditions that must be present in the therapeutic relationship: unconditional positive regard, genuineness, and empathy. Empathy means putting yourself in another person's shoes to see the world from his/her perspective. Well, I wish some other poor bugger had put my shoes on that day at Herringthorpe playing fields in 1971 and had run the sack race for me. I

176

continue to have nightmares about that day and still have panic attacks whenever I see a hessian sack.

When we were asked by the headmaster to stay on after school and participate in trials for the forth-coming sports day, you can imagine how thrilled the entire class of ten-year-olds felt. Having to remain for two extra hours within the confines of the school grounds with a complete competitive lunatic, pissed wet through, no tea inside our scrawny bellies, and the constant belittling of the less able athletes didn't quite float our boat.

Catholic schools excelled in discipline and more discipline, followed by regular thrashings and compulsory church attendance. Little time was ever spent nurturing athletic skills of the pupils, and coaching consisted of knocking every bit of self-belief out of you.

The school had no sports facilities other than a bald football pitch littered with dog turds. The only equipment we had were old sacks, a mouldy selec-tion of bean bags, and a few rickety hurdles. This, however, didn't put off our headmaster one jot. Sports Day was very important to him because we competed against another Catholic school where he'd once taught, which had overlooked him for the post of headmaster several years earlier. He was fiercely competitive towards St. Paul's and desperate for us to win the prestigious Vincent de Paul trophy. The truth of the matter was that our school was utterly and completely useless. We never won bugger all mainly because we were crap. It was as simple as that! Sometimes you can cleverly put spin on things and turn a loss into a victory—but when you had to deal with a complete set of losers, bereft of any talent whatsoever, it does make the task more difficult, if not impossible.

Every single person in my class despised this day with a passion. We accepted losing with great dignity, as if it were inevitable. The problems arose on the coach trip home when the Head went ballistic and crushed what tiny morsel of spirit we had out of us. He was a terrible loser and a tyrant. He would ridicule our lacklustre performance with a kind of smugness, telling us how good he used to be at our age and how many races he'd won. He was so far up his own arse when it came to bragging about his previous successes that his verbal diarrhoea engulfed us all in a sea of bullshit. He didn't inspire us with his tales of being a champion. On the contrary, he just made us feel even more inadequate.

The trials took place one Tuesday afternoon in the month of "Flaming June," meaning it was belting down with rain—such are summers in England. Bored beyond belief, soaked to the skin, and feeling totally pissed off, I was nominated by my teacher to try out for the sack race. **Why would anyone in their right mind want to race in a sack?** I remember thinking to myself at the time. When you put it into perspective it is ludicrous.

Against my better judgement, and not wanting to get "six of the best" across my arse with the headmaster's cane, I reluctantly agreed to participate. Because the hessian sack was so old and sodden wet through, when I managed to scramble into the aged bag at the starting line-up, my feet went straight through it. The sack then became a sort of dress with no bottom in it. Following the instruction of "Get ready," a loud **bang** resonated from the starter pistol, and I was off like a shot. Unlike all the other contestants, instead of hopping, I just kept the sack touching floor level to disguise the fact that my sack possessed no bottom in it and ran the entire race. I won by a mile, and through my cheating, was elected unanimously to represent the school the following week.

When Sports Day finally arrived, I was terrified. My devious ways in the trials had been my downfall, and here I was, standing inside a brand new sack, waiting for the gun to go off. This was the last race of the day, and miraculously, if I won, our school would take the coveted trophy for the first time in years. The stress and pressure I was under was unbearable. Added to this was the fact that half the bloody population of Maltby had travelled to Herringthorpe to support our school. I stared hard into the other competitors' eyes, desperately trying to psych them out, but to no avail. The lad to my right looked every inch an athlete, and to further compound my misery looked so cool, calm, and collected I could have died on the spot.

"He's the South Yorkshire champion at one hundred yards dash, javelin, hurdles *and* one mile sprint," said the boy to my immediate left.

One mile sprint? Holy shit, he must be good! There is no chance of me winning this piddling race with him in it. What was I to do? But before I could come up with a fiendish plan the starter gun went off, rocking me to my foundations. Everyone set off like demented springs, hopping wildly towards the finishing line. That was everyone except me. Instead of pulling the handles of the sack in an upwards direction and keeping my feet together to maintain a rhythmical hopping motion, I dropped back into my cheat mentality and tried to run. Big, big mistake. I moved all of three feet and fell forwards like a lead plummet, breaking my nose on impact with the ground. I can vaguely remember hearing the voluminous applause for the South Yorkshire champion and the sardonic chants of "prick" aimed in my direction.

Obscurity and anonymity beckoned me forth, and due to my lack of "fleetness of foot," I was about to be crucified by all and sundry. The only burning rubber I was going to experience was across the cheeks of my arse. I had been strong-minded and full of intent at the beginning of the race, but now I was only filled with shame.

The local priest sauntered over to me, and ignoring my plight and blood-stained clothing, uttered the comforting words of, "Hart, you slack twat."

I now realised that I was lower than a racing snake's belly when it came to the popularity stakes in our school and village. My only consolation was my close pal Dave, known as "Peapod," had witnessed my disastrous attempt in the race and fully understood my predicament. The hassle I was about to be subjected to from all quarters regarding my failure was going to be immense. Peapod helped me to my feet and escorted me to the changing rooms.

With blood still streaming down my face I heard Granny shouting, "You useless little wanker. You're a waste of space. Don't bother coming home, you fuck-wit."

These kind and reassuring words lifted my spirits somewhat, and I began to feel better. I needed a tonic. A tonic called REVENGE! Peapod sat me down alongside the lockers and shoved his handkerchief up my nose. Even though his intentions were good, the feeble little piece of soiled cotton proved no match for my blood. Suddenly, he alerted me to the fact that the winner's sports bag was next to where we were both sitting. The champion was on cloud nine, and during the delirious celebrations, he had inadvertently left his property in the changing rooms and gone off to proclaim his superiority to the rest of his classmates and family.

"Hey Alfie, why don't you use his shirt to mop up your blood, mate?" suggested Peapod.

"I've thought of something a little better than that my friend," I replied. "Pass me his bag."

Due to all the pressure I'd been under, followed by the pain of breaking my nose and the onslaught of abuse I'd received from well-wishers, I was feeling pretty shitty. So I whipped my shorts down and crapped in the winner's holdall, all over his clothes. For good measure, I wiped my backside on his shirt and dried my grubby hands on his coat. In collusion with my pal, I had exacted revenge on my opponent in the same way he had shit all over me in the race. Ah, the sweet smell of success!

I'll always remember Peapod for his help that day, and for being able to lie with the best of them when questioned by the police over the incident. He maintained total silence, took a beating for me off the headmaster, and was leathered by his dad for being mixed up with the likes of me.

Another thing I remember about Peapod was that years later, he came to visit me whilst I was doing my degree in Leeds. I decided to take him out for a curry with a few mates. The problem with Peapod was that he hadn't been out of Maltby in twenty years and had never been in a restaurant. Quite bizarrely, he insisted on wearing a nylon stocking over his head for the entirety of the meal giving the impression he was about to commit a crime. The only felony committed that night was that Peapod was allowed out beyond the hours of 7.00pm, and was mixing with the general public at large.

I ordered a vindaloo, along with my two mates. When the waiter asked Peapod what he wanted he said, "I can't stand wine, mate. I'll stick to a pint of beer."

There is a saying where I come from which goes as follows: You can take the man out of Maltby, but you can't take Maltby out of the man.

Whilst on the restaurant theme, I was recently out with my wife at an American diner on the outskirts of Sheffield. After perusing the menu, my wife ordered chicken fajitas. The waiter then asked my wife whether she wanted a salsa dip or a guacamole dip with her fajitas. My good lady chose the latter. Having taken our full order, the waiter then ran through our selection again in order to ensure he had heard us correctly.

"So, madam, you want guac on your fadge?" he recited.

Roughly translated into Yorkshire dialect, this means, "So missus, you want seminal fluid on your pussy?"

My wife looked deeply into the waiter's eyes and ingenuously replied, "Will it make it taste better?"

The taste of success always seemed to bypass me, even when accompanied with a small helping of guac. Sports days at school irritated the arse off me, but local sports competitions between rival gangs were entirely different. These were brilliant to take part in. No stupid races and collecting beanbags. No way. We played real games like archery, throwing arrows, board skating, and footie. These were games that made a lad feel proud to be in a team and remain constantly competitive. Coaching came from other fellow team members, and the mood was always positive and focused. The drive to be the best at these sports was massive, and rivalry was fierce yet fair. Boys and girls would come together on the local field, and battle would commence. Always organised by the older members of the respective gangs, these events were stage-managed so well even Harvey Goldsmith, the famous promoter, would have been proud.

Archery consisted of aiming arrows at a moving target halfway across the field, usually one of the mates' dogs or some little urchin nobody liked. Bows were handmade by different lads from ash trees, with twine or elastic linking the two ends to form a strong tension from which the arrows were propelled. The arrows were made from soft wood dowelling rods stolen from a local joinery firm. These were carefully split at the top, and cardboard flights were inserted. Cotton was wrapped around the top to secure the flights, and the other ends were sharpened into a point. The kid, or target, was then blindfolded and told to run around, never daring to stop for fear of a pounding from other gang members. The prey or target could only stop if directly hit by an archer. First to hit the target won.

Throwing arrows were also made from timber dowelling rods in the same way as the standard arrows, but instead of sharpening the ends into a point with a knife, we would securely fix the metal ends of darts by unscrewing the plastic tips first—this gave the throwing arrow a good weight. A strong piece of cord about three feet long was used as the launcher. This was tied at one end into several knots in order to form a clump or mass. The clump of knots was carefully placed on the arrow just under the tips and held down with the index finger whilst the remaining length of twine was wrapped around the arrow and over the knot. The cord was then pulled taught down the length of the arrow shaft until it reached the metal point. You then coiled the remainder of the twine around your hand and clenched your fist for a good grip. With arm outstretched, you ran about ten feet along the ground and launched the arrow skywards, releasing your hand from the base of the shaft. (It was similar to throwing a small spear combined with a dart.) If you mastered the technique correctly, these special hand-made projectiles would fly the length of a football pitch. (I would also like to point out that they could cause serious injury; my mate's ear, or lack of it, is testament to this!) The competition was simply who could throw the arrow the farthest.

Another sporting event we all loved was board skating, but not using the kind of board that they use today in skateboarding. Oh no. We'd get an old pair of roller skates and a piece of wood about two feet long by nine inches wide. The skates were nailed to the underside of the wood at each end. These purpose-made boards were great for moving in a straight line, but due to the lack of flexibility, cumbersome and dangerous when trying to turn corners. We would form a ramp about three feet high and start from the top of Black Hill. With a shove from one of your pals, you aimed for the ramp, and if successful, flew into the air like Eddie the Eagle. A referee would stand alongside the ramp and place a chalk mark on the road where you landed. On many occasions I witnessed the referee being taken out by a boarder who missed the ramp. We wore no protection, and it was commonplace for the competitors to limp home battered and bruised beyond belief. But back then, we were tough—or maybe just plain stupid.

The finale of the day's competition was the football match. As many as forty players could be on the pitch at one time, and the rule book was thrown out the window. Football boots were a must, due to the actual football being made of a cross between leather and cast iron. If it was raining on the big day, and the ball got wet, no person would have the strength to kick it more than a few yards. No one ever thought about heading it when it rained, for fear of ending up looking like the cricketer Gladstone Small—who is minus a neck! These games were highly competitive and no prisoners were taken. If you were fouled by a member of the opposition, however hard the tackle was, you didn't whinge and roll about on the floor like these modern nancy-boy soccer players. You'd just get up and run off the injury. If you dared to moan, you were slagged off by all the other players and supporters, including your own team members. Worse still, you were labelled a puff.

I remember a kid called Neil Kennedy who walked up to me just before the kick-off and wellied me on the shin. He then told me that this was an act of "pre-venge". When I asked him what this meant, he informed me it was his way of doling out his retribution on me, prior to me fouling him in the game. This made perfect sense to me at the time, and I've still got the scar to prove it. It was also common practice for some of the parents and grandparents to join in—such was the thirst for winning.

One gentleman called Wack Walker, in his mid-fifties, would regularly participate in the game. He wore hobnail leather boots which were crafted and manufactured by Orcs from Tolkien's *Lord of the Rings*. He would race onto the pitch halfway through the game, unleash his right boot under a small child, and send it hurtling skywards. He also had a knack of kicking the ball really hard into kids' faces, dislodging teeth in the process. Child abuse wasn't intended, the man didn't mean any harm—he simply wanted his team to win. I still thank God, and my dentist, that he was always on my side during the games.

Unlucky Alf

I once remember some arsehole of a spectator heckling him in a game. Old Man Walker stopped the game and put his foot over the ball. The world stopped for a few seconds and silence descended on and around the pitch. He looked up in the direction of the heckler and said, "I don't come to your place of enjoyment and ask you to take your cock out of his arse, do I?"

Following the match, Mr Walker walked over to this particular guy and knocked him clean out with one punch. No one messed with Mr Walker—fact!

Chapter 23

Pastures New

In 1972, we moved house from my Grandmother's to a section of Maltby known as Cliff Hills. This was considered a more affluent part of the village—where you could shut the windows without trapping someone's hands as they were trying to break in. They say moving house is one of the most stressful things a person has to deal with in life, but when you're eleven years old it's great. The smell of untreated timber and new plaster filled the air as we entered the three-bedroom semi-detached house on Redwood Drive. To add to the excitement, I quickly noticed that our new back garden looked onto a wood and a working quarry. Craig and I were allocated a back bedroom which overlooked the small wood and the quarry, and from our elevated vantage point I could carry out my bird watching.

It was around this time that my interest in gardening began to grow, which is something I'm still extremely fond of to this day. The gardens at our new house were barren of any life other than a sparse selection of weeds. I took it on myself to dig both the front and back gardens immediately, to try to make our house more attractive to the neighbours. This I did with a small hand trowel and it took me an age. With blistered hands and a broken back I was completely knackered, but it was my first taste of accomplishment, a real achievement. I love the odour of new soil as it is quarried from the earth and turned over to face the sunlight—deep brown-coloured earth, freshly tilled and smelling wonderful. Such was my joy the day I completed our garden, I picked up a sample of soil and ate it, out of respect. You should try it sometime, preferably when no one is looking. It tasted surprisingly rich and earthy!

By this stage of my life I fully accepted that we were poor. Even though we had just recently moved into a new house, we still didn't own it—Maltby Council did. Back then we used to have a rent collector, who turned up every fortnight to collect his dues. Invariably we didn't have enough cash to pay him, so we would hide behind the sofa with Mum until he became bored of knocking on the front door and went away. On one occasion, the rent man had seen Craig and I running into the house from one of the neighbour's gardens and chased after us with all the speed the old git could muster. We knew the drill and immediately hid behind the settee whilst my mother locked the door. The rent collector started hammering on the door, nearly breaking the inset glass panel, shouting at the top of his voice that he'd seen us and demanding my Mum answered the door. He then decided to bend down and open the letter box. The glass panel in our front door was frosted, so visibility was poor. Now with the letter box wide open, he could see straight into the hallway and listen for any movement or sound. He carried on shouting into the aperture, asking if anyone was present in the house.

Suddenly, without any prompting Craig shouted back to the man from our hiding place, "My mother has told us to tell you she's not in."

From nowhere, a slipper came hurtling through the air and hit Craig straight in the face, sending him flying backwards towards the front window. As he stumbled, he grabbed the curtains to steady him, causing the entire pelmet and curtains, along with the inset net curtains, to be ripped from their fixings and thus exposing our entire front room. The noise of the commotion alerted the rent man who suddenly appeared at the window. Quick as a flash, my Mum whispered from behind the arm chair to lay flat to the floor and pretend we were dead. We both did exactly what she said and lay down motionless, not daring to move a muscle or blink an eye. After several seconds, Craig asked my Mum through clenched teeth so as not to draw attention to himself, why we were pretending to be dead. My Mum whispered back that we were just rehearsing—she would kill us both later! She never did answer the door that day, and fortunately the rent man died the following week, from a stress-related illness.

After spending a few weeks in our new abode, we decided to start venturing farther afield beyond the adjoining woods into the surrounding countryside. We came across a turnip field laden with large purple vegetables ripe for eating and stealing. Within two days we'd established a little business selling turnips to the neighbours for a small profit. We set off at first light armed with sacks and filled them to the brim. The sacks were then placed on our homemade trolley and carted home to be "topped and tailed" and scrubbed clean. The turnips were then put in smaller clear bags and sold to any willing buyer. This carried on for several weeks, and business was starting to look up. We'd met some new friends, and quickly they were employed to help our little enterprise grow. This was my first entrepreneurial experience, and one in which I revelled. I know that stealing is wrong, but when you are skint, needs must.

A major rule when stealing is CYA. (Cover Your Arse.) Never leave any evidence—oh, and don't be greedy. Just take what you need. The farmer's field

189

in which the turnips grew was massive, and instead of taking the loot from one area, we carefully spread our spoils across the entire field so as not to draw the farmer's attention to our pilfering. To further trick our victim, we placed a couple of rabbit carcasses in one area of the field, an old burnt-out motorbike in another, and made a small fire with hay bales in yet another. We thought that these little surprises would make the farmer think that the thieving bastards who had stolen part of his crop would be older boys. Our thriving business came to an abrupt halt when Craig sold two turnips to my pious and strict aunt. When she realised that the goods were a little "warm," she summoned my mother to her house and read her the riot act. My mother of course denied all knowledge of our exploits and promised to chastise us severely on her return home. Fortunately on this particular occasion, she didn't carry out her punishment. She'd benefited greatly from our illegal spoils, being in on 85% of the profits...

The day after we'd closed the business down, Craig and I were out walking when we noticed the farmer on his tractor in the turnip field. To our sheer amazement, he began to plough the entire and remaining turnip crop back into the ground. What madness were we witnessing? All this stock going to waste. When we returned home, out of embarrassment and sadness, we made a pact not to tell anyone what we had just seen.

Moving to a new area presented us with new opportunities. Just down the road from where we lived was a football pitch, belonging to a local knitwear firm, called Byford's Field. The firm's soccer team only played on it every alternate Saturday so the rest of the time it was used by the local kids. The best thing about the pitch was that it was regularly cut and maintained and therefore provided an excellent play area for all concerned. The only downside to allowing local access was that most of the irresponsible dog owners in the vicinity used to allow their dogs to foul all over it; this also included my Mum. It's not pleasant to be halfway through a critical game of football and when tackled from behind fall head first into a pile of fresh, warm dog shit, deposited by some canine that very morning—even if that canine belongs to you!

The field also provided a wide open space for children to run around in and release excess energy. It never fails to amaze me how many school football pitches across the land stand idle all year round—the ones in my neighbourhood included. These spaces should be opened up to local kids in order to give them somewhere to go on summer evenings and weekends. It would be a meeting place where they could burn off their pent up frustrations and be able to mix and interact with other kids. Emphasis would be placed on getting fit and staying fit whilst injecting fun and competitiveness. The government should build onto schools purpose-made facilities where children can get changed and showered. And yes, they should be supervised by qualified staff at all times. The youth of today are our future, and we must nurture them. We should give children incentives to exercise more often and be made to feel part of a team and feel part of their community. The kids should have access to trained coaches in all aspects of sports and be taught the importance of staying healthy. (*Mens sana in corpore sano*—healthy body, healthy mind.) If you're wondering where all the money would come from to put these suggestions in place, it's no good asking me. I've no fucking idea. I'm not a politician or an economist. If you know one, ask them. I'm just an ideas person.

One of my favourite activities on Byford's Field was kite flying, which isn't by any stretch of the imagination really classed as a sport. But it does involve short bursts of running in the open air. It also does help if it's windy—or getting the actual kite off the ground and into the air can prove extremely difficult and frustrating. When I was growing up, no one bought a kite, we made our own, relying on resourcefulness.

Kite flying was a regular sight in my youth, both with kids *and* grown-ups. Making your own kite cost next to bugger all, so everyone had them. Some more inventive and more adept parents made their children box kites, but being limited in my kite-making skills, I always opted for the standard type of kite. They flew as high and were just as good. When a decent blustery day came along, you would find masses of kids on our field flying their respective handmade kites. If you've ever experienced the thrill of flying an ordinary kite—or any type of kite for that matter—it's a wonderful feeling because, for some strange reason it makes you laugh. I have no idea why, but it does. I love to laugh for no apparent reason as I think it makes it even funnier—but flying a kite simply brings a smile to your face, followed by a spontaneous laugh. If you don't believe me, try it sometime … you know you want to!

Another innocent and funny little game we would play whilst flying our kites was called "aerial messages." We would get an approximately three inch square piece of thin card and write a personal message on it, like a wish or something. A small nick in the card was then made and this was slipped onto the bottom of

192

the main kite string just above the handle. The wind would then catch hold of the card and send it spiralling upwards towards the kite itself. So in actual fact, you were sending an aerial message to your kite, asking it to grant your requests. Completely stupid and point-less I know, but it made us happy back then because we believed in the "power of the kite". Limited intel-ligence can be limiting. I once sent my kite a message asking for a bigger penis, but the card dislodged itself from the main string and blew away. And because the kite didn't receive the message, unfortunately I'm still stuck with a twelve-inch cock!

Chapter 24

Bikes, Brakes, and Bruises

The experience of moving from the working class in one part of Maltby, to the more affluent working class in another area, showed me that a lot of what we understand as class is as much in our minds as in our pockets. Where I came from, people voted by what they had in their pockets—in our case, we had nowt.

Hard work never hurt anyone, and if you have a job with a low wage, you need to do something about it. Betterment for yourself and your family is important; and valuing what you've earned and using it wisely can make a big difference in your life and those close to you.

When I left college to start my first job, I realised that to get ahead, I would need to earn more. So I worked harder in my main job and took another one on in the evenings and over the weekend. I have always lived within my means and never been a borrower or a moaner. To me, if you want something badly enough you have to earn it in the best way you know how—and my best way has been through hard work combined with talent. Hard work is an ethic, and talent comes with practice. However bad their situation is, people sometimes prefer to stay in their comfort zone because they cannot see beyond the box they live in, or simply don't want to.

I used to hang out with a lad called Mac, whose family situation was just like ours—skint! But one

Christmas morning, Mac came to call for me on his new bike—a Raleigh Chopper—a kid's bike manufactured in the 1970s by the Raleigh Company of Nottingham. Possessing a unique style and design which set it apart from all other bicycles at that time, the Chopper became an instant success and a classic cult item—a must-have, and the epitome of cool. The bike had a distinct customized design similar to a chopper motorcycle made popular by the movie '*Easy Rider*'—the 1969 film starring drugged-up, laid back bikers Peter Fonda and Dennis Hopper. They headed out on the highway in search of America. It quickly received cult status, a leader in "road movies" and a landmark flick that spoke to a disaffected generation of people. I considered myself as something of a rebel, like Fonda.

The original Chopper Mk1 was initially launched in America in 1968 but failed to take off. When it was released in Britain in 1970, it took off like a rocket. The things that impressed me so much about this revolutionary bike were its long padded seat, backrest, and iconic Ape Hanger handle bars. Due to its length, the seat positively encouraged "backies," where two people travelled on the bike at the same time. Now health and safety boffins would be all over this design like a rash. It has since been modified and re-launched. The Chopper also had a 3-speed gear hub, which operated like a car gear system by having a frame-mounted chunky gear lever. It boasted different size wheels front and back and had wider tyres than standard bikes of that time.

All in all, it was a sensation, and Mac blew my bollocks off that day. It was the very first time I had been in total awe of something. I wanted to worship it.

Due to the heavy steel frame and lack of stability, the Chopper did have its problems. It promoted itself as a taxi, due to the size of the seat and, the driver was forced more forwards when giving passengers lifts. Many a boy had his groin walloped on the gear stick at one time or another. When riding a Chopper, you couldn't muster up fast speeds—but you did look cool.

Mac's Chopper cost a whopping £32.00, which was a small fortune back then—about a week's wage. His dad was a miner at the local colliery and his Mum a cleaner at school. I often wondered how his parents could afford such luxuries until Mac explained that his Mum had four different jobs, in addition to a mothering three kids and looking after the house. Mrs Mac was a workhorse who had set her sights on buying her lad a brand new must-have bike, without affecting the state of the family expenses. She was a smashing woman who died young, probably because of too much work and not enough rest, however, set an example to me about having a strong work ethic, which still remains to this day.

Seeing Mac's Chopper (his bike, not his penis) made me realise that my dreams of owning something new were exactly that—only dreams. I've never been a jealous person, but I do have to admit that on seeing him on his cool machine, I did wish instant death on him. Knowing I hadn't a chance in hell of ever getting a new bike, you can imagine my total surprise on coming home from school one evening and being presented with my own bike! It was third-hand and missing a few fundamental items like a seat, but it was mine. My mother had purchased the bicycle from one of our neighbours who apparently was about to throw it away. I subsequently found out that she had paid £5.00, which was quite expensive for something that was on its way to the dump.

Even though the bike looked ugly and old, it was better than walking, so I set about restoring it to its former glory. I found an old seat (minus the cover), and my Grandad tied one of his old flat caps over the springs, which made the bike look even more ridiculous but slightly less uncomfortable. The tyres were blown up to the correct pressure, and after a good polish, I was off on the road with Mac. The makeshift seat did provide an excellent talking point with my mates, but after a while, people stopped laughing and I was accepted as a proper cyclist. My first big excursion was to Roche Abbey, but Grandad insisted on me passing my Cycling Proficiency Test prior to this, which I did with flying colours, having had only two lessons and achieving 96%.

Mac called for me early one Saturday morning and off we set, two pioneers seeking new adventures around every corner. We made great time on the outward journey, and I have to admit that my excuse for a bike was far faster than its opponent, the Chopper. On arriving at the abbey, we each did a quick "gypsy kiss" behind some bushes and then remounted to set off home—there seemed no point in hanging around when we could be hurtling along the highway.

Our homeward journey was something to look forward to as it allowed us to freewheel down a large hill, near the village of Stone. Here we could pick up speed, and then take our feet off the pedals and let the steep incline and the bike's forward momentum do the work. With excitement etched across our little faces, we raced to the summit and whizzed down the lane like bullets. I can still remember looking over to Mac and seeing him howling with laughter as the wind whistled through his blonde hair. As our speed increased, Mac shouted to me to check my brakes in case of an emergency. He suggested I do this very carefully by gradually increasing pressure on my metal levers to ensure my bicycle responded, and then begin to decelerate. If I'd have applied the brakes too sharply, I'd fly straight over the handle bars. I nodded, agreeing to his instructions and gingerly touched my brakes. No response whatsoever. I applied more pressure, ever mindful of the potential speed I was achieving at this point of the journey. Again nothing happened. I looked over to Mac and suddenly noticed that he was now some way behind me.

At this stage I began to feel desperate and started to worry. I squeezed the brake levers as hard as I could, praying for the bike to start behaving itself and respond to my actions, but alas—nothing. It just seemed to make me go even faster. Panic was now setting in, and the colour of adrenalin was definitely dark brown. What on earth was I to do? Mac was now out of earshot, and on looking down at where my brake pads should have been, I realised that I actually didn't possess any. Instead of the connection of rubber to metal, it was metal on metal. This didn't look good, and I began to fear the worst. What did fate hold in store for me? I've always had a low pain threshold, and here I was facing probable death.

I cannot remember thinking anything else after this point on my *ride of doom,* as I smashed straight into the back of a parked trailer and was instantly rendered unconscious. Thirty minutes later, I came round to the odour of smelling salts being administered by the local farmer's wife. I was somewhat dazed and couldn't focus properly, but gradually managed to move my legs and arms. This was followed by my head and then the rest of my body. Thank the lord! Nothing broken, only my fall, which had been cushioned by straw that had been the cargo of the trailer I'd smashed into the back of.

Lying there gazing into the eyes of the lady, I became aware that her hand was between my legs. This didn't feel right, and I thought to myself, *What kind of dirty bastard is she?*

The woman in question then rummaged under my groin and retrieved her false teeth. My mind had now gone into overdrive, but I could clearly see that my jeans were buckled up.

The woman swiftly repositioned her dentures into her mouth and said, "Seeing you lying unconscious betwixt the straw, I decided to give you the kiss of life. When I bent down and opened my mouth, my false teeth fell out into your lap. Sorry about that. Anyway, you look all right to me now so let's be having you home."

Narrow escape by all accounts, I thought at the time. What would have been worse: instant death, or being tongued by an old fart? (Answers on a postcard please.)

In addition to my lucky encounter with the trailer full of straw, I can recount another less fortunate incident I happened to be involved in, the following week. I was happily chatting to a group of mates, trying to impress a girl I'd had my eye on who was standing on the other side of the road. She was pretending to take no notice of me, even when I started trying to stand on my hands and spit through the gap in my front teeth. Such was my debonair style and class—I thought I was the ultimate cool dude.

Getting nowhere with her, I decided to take the bull by the horns and go over to where she was standing and talk to her face to face. Plucking up the courage, I ventured onto the road, only to be hit from behind by a boy called Duke who happened to be riding his Chopper. To add insult to injury, he just laughed in my face—not a word of apology did he utter to me. His Chopper was bedecked with two large flagpoles on the back and covered with tassels, which he thought made him look even cooler. He also fancied this same girl.

When he had deliberately crashed into me, my arse got trapped between his mudguard and tyre, and I can tell you it hurt like hell. Looking up at his smug face, desperately trying to stop a torrent of tears from cascading down my cheeks, I realised there was no confusion in my mind—only thoughts of revenge. The culpability lay fair and square at his doorstep. My backside was burning like a furnace, and I hatched a plan there and then to square matters up between us. His lack of manners and nastiness needed to be sorted, once and for all. This calamity could have been easily averted, but he chose to humiliate me in front of everyone and the hostility between us now ran deeper than the Grand Canyon. Slowly picking myself up, I hobbled home, not daring to look back at my mates or my beloved, for fear of major embarrassment.

The following day, a bike race around our block had been arranged by some older lads. The race was to take place at 5 p.m. and would consist of twenty laps. Back then few people owned cars so the roads were a lot less congested and safer. Cars were not as fast, and drivers didn't try to break the speed limits as much. Duke turned up just before the race was to commence, but to my amazement, he wasn't on his Yellow Peril. Instead he sat proudly astride his elder brother's racer. That same smug look was written all over his face as he beamed his pearly whites at me.

The girl we both fancied also happened to be there, darting her eyes across at both of us, trying hard not to look too interested, but inwardly delighted that two boys were about to compete for her affections.

I knew there and then that I didn't stand a hope in hell of winning so I pretended to twist my ankle just as I was about to mount my rusty steed. Edgar, the race organiser, halted proceedings to check my injury. He decided that I was to be removed from the race, though I was just trying to win over my girl with an Oscar performance of play-acting as there was really nothing wrong with me. All competitors said how sorry they felt for me—all except one—Duke. He was too busy up his own arse to even acknowledge me. I hobbled over to Jane, limping like a war veteran, and to my complete astonishment, she put her arm around me for comfort. On seeing this spontaneous act of real affection, Duke went blood red with anger. I felt I'd already won the race for Jane.

Edgar sounded his horn, and the race was on. Thirty riders jostled for position, several of whom fell off after a few yards. Around the first bend they raced out of sight of the spectators. By now I'd lost all interest in the race and had my eyes firmly fixed on Jane's cleavage, which for a girl of twelve, was magnificent as far as I was concerned. She smelt beautiful, and I can pinpoint my first erection at this junction in my life—and boy, did it feel good. Mind you, several hours later, still with the same erection and a severe case of blue balls, I must say that I didn't feel the same way!

To my utter disgust, Duke was leading the field on the nineteenth lap, and Jane turned her attention to him. What was I to do? There's no way that I could possibly allow him to win. On his final lap with the finishing line in sight, Duke was well ahead of the other competitors, smiling like a Cheshire cat.

I need to teach that cocky twat a lesson, I thought, and in a flash of brilliance, I picked up a tennis ball from the ground and threw it just in front of his bike.

As luck would have it, it wedged in the spokes on his front wheel and jammed in the mud flap bringing him to a sudden and instant halt. He performed a magnificent handstand whilst still gripping the handlebars, and then was catapulted forwards at the speed of sound into a stationary car. With the grace and elegance of a rhinoceros, he tumbled onto the road and lay motionless. Everyone ran to his aid— everyone but me. I was off like a shot, forgetting my limp and my bike in the process. For all I was concerned, he could be dead. Revenge was sweet; but I lost my girl when she ended up comforting Duke for the remainder of the night. That same girl went on to be a nurse, and is now a foreign diplomat. She doesn't know what really happened that night as it was getting dark as the race neared the end. She missed out on marrying a sneaky, cowardly bastard— but that's her loss, not mine.

Chapter 25

Quarry Rafting

Just a stone's throw behind our house, a wonderful working quarry was situated, which provided bricks for the building industry. Because it was a working concern and its operation carried out blasting on a daily basis, it was deemed private property. The quarrying of the clay took place during the daytime, as did the blowing up of the rocks. But by 5 p.m. the place was deserted, apart from a night watchman who seldom ever ventured out of his hut at the far end of the site. Obviously, even our little gang was not stupid enough to enter the quarry during working hours, but come the evening when it was empty of diggers and men, it became our turf.

The quarry itself was massive, especially through the eyes of children like us. Its steep-sided banks enclosed the grounds, towering over deep turquoise lagoons, and providing excellent play facilities for us. We were completely oblivious to the potential danger we faced. Our parents never had a clue as to our whereabouts and naturally never suspected the risks we were taking.

Such was the weird landscape and the enormity of this gigantic hole in the ground that whenever we entered the site, it was as if we were transported into a different dimension, on another planet. A geologist's dream and a child's fairytale. When you stood at ground level bang in the centre of this hole, you felt insignificant and small. The sheer scale of the cliffs and the vastness of the quarry itself were difficult to fully take in.

My wife had a similar feeling when we visited New York. She felt claustrophobic on the busy streets, shrouded on all sides by huge buildings blanking out the sunlight and the sky. She said she was overwhelmed and in awe of the colossal scale of the architecture and the sharp rise of the buildings, which seemed to go on forever. Trying to fathom the actual height of these structures gave her a *neck breaker* feeling and made her feel nauseous. She likened it to how a small insect views our world, and how inconsequential we are in the whole scheme of things.

When I am confronted with such a monumental manmade expanses or massive structures, the only thing that springs to mind are the words "fuck me" which is obviously a reflection on my intellect.

Going into this hole in the ground was like taking a journey to the centre of the earth—scary, yet exciting. The deep, clear waters catered to our swimming needs, and being free made the experience even more exhilarating.

Nowadays if children were found trespassing on private property in a working quarry, Health and Safety officials would go apeshit, and the entire grounds would be fenced off, with CCTV cameras installed around the entire perimeter. Back then CCTV didn't exist, and when I think about it, neither did perimeter fencing. If you went at the right time, you could just walk into the quarry unchallenged.

We would play on our makeshift rafts in the quarry pools for hours during the summer months. These floating structures were made from three thick sheets of polystyrene (about four feet long by three feet wide by three inches thick). The polystyrene was provided courtesy of one of the local firms that never locked its store correctly. Three lightweight sheets were held together with used welding rods, also provided by a local welding company—they also never secured their property. The rods were poked through the polystyrene around the outer edges, and hey presto, the raft was made. Due to the lightness of the vessel, it could be easily transported. We would usually make two rafts, each raft holding two kids.

Occasionally on one of the many ponds within the quarry, we'd play "Battleships" and try to dislodge the other team with bricks and other missiles. During these escapades, to provide extra excitement, other gang members would stand on the sidelines and also throw huge boulders around our rafts and try to create authentic battle conditions. It did generate bloody big waves and made loud thumping and splashing noises. Many a child got severely injured by some of the larger missiles, but few ever complained because if they did, they would be tortured by the rest of the gang. (Rules were rules.) We'd use cricket bats to paddle our vessels, which could also be used to knock opponents off *their* respective rafts. Each battle never lasted longer than forty seconds—such was the intensity of the aerial bombardments and violent confrontations. Warfare was always carried out in the spirit of fun, leaving the green waters muddied by our blood.

Around the outskirts of the quarry, several well established ponds could be found, all boasting a wealth of newts. "Newting" was a superb way of spending a day, and when you caught one of these beautiful creatures, it filled you with a sense of wonder. Catching and transporting newts is now a criminal offence, following the introduction of the 1981 UK Wildlife and Countryside Act. But when I was a lad, no such law had been introduced so we captured thousands of the little buggers, and transported them everywhere:

to school, church, shopping, and in my brother's case, to bed.

The species of newts found in our local vicinity were the Smooth Newt (*Triturus Vulgaris*) and the Great Crested Newt (*Triturus Cristatus*). The Smooth Newt is the most common of our three newts on the mainland of Great Britain. It lives in ponds during the spring and summer months, then moves to land, where it hibernates from mid October until February. The Great Crested Newt is the largest European newt and is much more conspicuous than the Smooth Newt. It has a distinctive warty skin and a vivid underbelly colour of yellowy-orange. We used to mistakenly refer to these newts as salamanders and, due to their size, would delight in catching them. The males can be distinguished from the females by the presence of a jagged crest running along their backs. My Grandad reckoned they could live up to one hundred years old, but he was an inveterate liar. They can actually live up to fifteen years old, which isn't too bad in the newting world and, come to think of it, is probably equivalent to a hundred human years. The female lays between two and three hundred eggs on aquatic plants in the ponds, which frogs find very tasty. The juvenile newts do get their own back on the frog's offspring by devouring young tadpoles. Such is nature's fine balance.

When I observe a newt close up, my mind is instantly transported back to the times when dinosaurs ruled the earth. Like crocodiles, these creatures have been around for millions of years and are amazing little critters. Unlike crocodiles, they don't actually bite, so they are much more user friendly. Grown-ups used to tell their children that if they handled newts they would catch warts, and like many kids I believed them, and still do to this day. Though this belief was once questioned whilst I was at college when a roommate told me he had got penal warts. Why he put a newt down his undercrackers was beyond me—some folks are crazy!

Another form of fishing carried out in the quarry was angling for explosive wire, which I know sounds rather bizarre. Due to the extraction of rock and clay, the quarrymen carried out controlled explosions on a regular basis. You could always tell when a blasting was about to take place because a loud alarm, which could be heard for miles, would go off. The red and yellow wires used to connect the explosive device to the detonator were found littered all over the quarry floor. I think reels of the stuff were also cast into the ponds for our enjoyment as there seemed no other logical explanation. We would locate a large length of this wire and attach a sharp stone by wrapping the excess wire tightly around it. This acted as the hook. The remaining wire would be coiled in one hand and held firmly, and the stone cast into the water and trawled along the bottom with the hope of retrieving another ball of wire submerged on the pond bed. This was easily achieved when the waters were clear, but after several attempts to try to hook the bundles the sediments in the water would be stirred up, making it resemble pea soup. This was one game I absolutely loved, but to this day I could not give you a reason why. Recently I was reminiscing with my brother about this futile and seemingly mindless game, trying to find rhyme or reason why we played it.

When I asked him why we enjoyed it so much, he replied, "There *was* no actual point in the game at all; but wasn't it brilliant!"

The quarry waters also provided a place to teach a dog to swim. Somewhere along the way, we had managed to acquire another two dogs, as Kesh was now getting on a bit. These two mongrels wandered into the back kitchen one day and adopted us on the spot. They were both young dogs, less than a year old. I took it upon myself to teach them hunting skills, and the first lesson was swimming. The dogs had terrier in them, which was quite obvious from their appearance. I had to find out if they had any other hunting qualities like ratting and retrieving instincts, which invariably involved water.

I trundled off to the quarry one morning with the two dogs excitedly snapping at my heels. On arriving at our destination, I grabbed hold of Teddy, the fluffier and more gormless of the pooches, and hurled him into the deep, clear water of one of the pools. To my utter amazement, he sank straight to the bottom, and just remained there, six feet under water and bolt upright. After what seemed like an eternity, as the hound wasn't actually doing anything, I dived into the lagoon fully dressed and retrieved him. When I reached the bank and hauled him onto dry land, he frantically shook himself dry, cocked his back leg up, and pissed down my sodden wet jeans. It was obvious to me that my teaching technique needed tweaking somewhat.

Second time around with Sam, our other dog, I tried a different approach. I stripped down to my undies and dived into the water, shouting his name as I went. Looking very agitated, he started whining and barking whilst pacing the water's edge. I carried on swimming to the other side of the lagoon, still calling and whistling to him. The dog became even more wound up and finally leapt like a gazelle into the water, landing smack on my back. He then proceeded to sink his teeth into my neck, like he was savaging a piece of meat. I swiftly walloped him off, and we both swam towards dry ground. I deemed this a great success due to the fact that Sam had demonstrated two things to me: he could swim and attack prey. As the years went on, he turned out to be a fabulous hunting dog.

What of Teddy? I hear you asking yourselves. I think he's still on the bottom of the pond bed, waiting to be rescued again!

Chapter 26
The Kissing Den

During my fourteenth year, two significant things happened to me that changed my life, and looking back, I realise that I'm still suffering acutely from both of them: the female sex and hay fever.

The effects of hay fever can vary greatly from individual to individual. Some sufferers have a mild case, where just their nasal passages block slightly for a while, whilst others have numerous symptoms from wheezing to conjunctivitis. Being blessed with hardly any luck, I fall into the category of having *all* the nasty symptoms that are associated with hay fever. These include sneezing fits, seasonal asthma, itchy throat, runny nose, etc.

I positively dread the period from the middle of June until the end of July. Even when it's pissing down with rain, if it falls between these dates, I'm fucked good and proper. Mornings and evenings are worst for me, but the remainder of the day is also crap. I've tried potions and lotions—all to no avail. I was even told as a teenager by my doctor that by the time I reached forty, I would have grown out of it. That never happened. On the contrary, I think I've grown into it. Each year it seems to get a little worse, and I've come to accept that I'll never get rid of it. In the war against hay fever, I have lost.

Hay fever is caused by pollen from certain plants. One of the first tree species to start releasing its arsenal onto the unsuspecting public is the London plane tree, which sets the ball rolling as early as March.

Dene Lindley

Hay fever is particularly prevalent during the month of June, when the grass pollens kick in—just in case you happen to be immune to the trees. I was the first person in our family to develop this dreaded allergy so I got very little support or sympathy from my nearest and dearest.

They say that the best form of prevention is to remain inside your house with the windows and doors securely fastened for the duration of the hay fever season. Trying to stop a kid from playing outside with his mates during the summer months is an impossible task. As a sufferer, even now, I still like to be outside just in case I miss the one warm summer day that we occasionally have in Britain. I'll put up with the symptoms just to feel the sunshine on my face. I never actually see the sunshine though, as my eyes are welded shut due to severe conjunctivitis caused by the hay fever—but the family tells me it's great.

Dealing with an allergy like hay fever is bad enough, but when it comes to the fairer sex, I must admit that I don't cope as well as most. If the truth be told, I'm a complete clusterfuck. It's always been the same for me, lurching from one disastrous relationship to another. Thank God when my wife finally found me on the end of a bar chewing a bone, she felt sorry for me and saw beyond what other people had. From a very early age, I've always been attracted to females, and as time ticks on, I still find myself flirting with the best of them. It never goes beyond the flirting stage because if it did, I'd crap myself, and my wife said she would cut off my testicles and shove them up my arsehole. Like most men though, I still look and dream.

Returning to my story—as Christmas was approaching in the year of 1974, I began to notice

211

that my body was changing. Every morning when I awoke, my cock was rock hard for no apparent reason. It would stay like this for an hour or so and create me no end of embarrassment at the breakfast table, eating my cornflakes. (I don't mean my cock was eating my cornflakes, as that would be ridiculous—it preferred sugar puffs.)

On noticing my bulge, my mother once said, "The only erect cock I want to see in a morning at the breakfast table is the one on the packet, you dirty little twat."

It suddenly dawned on me that I should now begin to come to breakfast fully clothed with the wee missile strapped down with my snake belt. I also noticed that strange, black curly hairs had begun sprouting down below, which looked rather bizarre to me as everywhere else on my body was as bald as a pig's throat.

What is happening to me? I wondered.

My question was answered the following day on the way to school, by an older boy called Dougal.

Dougal informed me that I was going through "the change". He had gone through the same process a year earlier, and his Mum was still going through it. He told me not to worry and to expect more "bars on" (erections) as I got older—he was certainly right on the money with that. To alleviate the erection problem, he graphically described to me the art of "spanking the monkey," or masturbation, as it is more commonly known. He went into great detail to explain exactly what happened and that the end result was magnificent.

All through my school lessons that day, my mind was on my new hobby, and I couldn't wait to get home and give it a try. That evening, I ran all the way home, complete with a tumid member, recalling all that Dougal had taught me that same morning. I ran straight upstairs and into the bathroom, locking the door as I had been instructed. My Mum shouted to me from downstairs, asking if I'd got the shits, but I was too preoccupied to answer her. Fifteen seconds later, I had mastered the art of pleasuring myself, and it felt unbelievable. So much so, I did it another three times—but as it went on, it took longer to reach the same state of ecstasy.

In my pursuit of pleasure, I found myself spending more and more time in the bathroom "bashing the bishop," which the female readers amongst you may find disgusting. The male readers, however, will now be feeling rather embarrassed knowing that I've alerted their female counterparts to what goes on when they're locked in the bathroom for hours. It was only when Dougal told me that if you masturbated too much you would go blind, scaring the life out of me so that I decided to limit my actions, choosing alternate days, to minimise the risk. When I asked him how he knew this, he told me that his dad had walked into his bedroom and caught him choking his chicken. His father told him to stop as it would make him go blind.

Dougal responded by saying, "Dad, I'm over here!"

Not really understanding that Dougal was "pissing up my back and telling me that it was raining," I believed him. Dougal went on to further my sexual education by explaining the female body in detail and how it worked. This fascinated me even more than indulging with the "five fingered widow," and he went on to say that when I reached the ripe old age of fourteen, my cock would turn into a magnet for female fannies. He finished off his tutorial by telling me that eventually I would grow up and "release the beast and let thousands of tadpoles out for a swim."

At this last statement, I was feeling rather confused. What the fuck was he saying to me? None of this made any sense whatsoever. Why do kids, who know nothing about sex, tell other more innocent kids a pack of lies when it comes to sexual education? On my way home from school the following day, I desperately tried to comprehend how in my coming years I would be "releasing the tadpoles for a beasting," but it just made my brain hurt. To think of nicer, easier topics and to help me carry out my mind shift, I decided that when I arrived home I would have a good "ham shank". This always made me feel better inside and cleared my head.

I once remember a big boy shouting at me across the road when I was going for a stroll with my Grandad. He called me a "Wanker," and I asked Grandad what it meant. He stopped dead in his tracks, took a long, hard look at me and said, "Don't worry about what it means son. In time you'll become an *expert* wanker."

I hadn't a clue what he was talking about at the time, but now, well into my forties, I am well on my way to achieving expert status.

One October morning, I was stopped by an older girl who lived at the bottom of my street. She asked me if I would be interested in building a den. I immediately agreed, as I thought myself a bit of a champion when it came to den construction. The girl's name was Lynn, and she was fifteen years old, which nearly made her a full woman in my eyes. She had blonde hair and beautiful skin, and on gazing into her eyes, I found myself falling head over heels in love with her. This fluctuation of fortune was too much for me to take in, and I found myself pinching my arm in order to snap me out of this heavenly dream. Nothing like this had ever happened to me before so I also had feelings of doubt racing through my mind. Something was bound to go wrong, like the world ending or my cock falling off.

Lynn introduced me to her friend Lucy, and we set off to the woods to begin work on the den. On the way, we met several other boys who all joined us, and one hour later the den was complete. It was superb by anyone's reckoning and Lynn and her friend looked delighted with the finished product. All the boy gang members tried to pile into the den, but Lynn insisted that she and Lucy be the only ones going in. The rest of us would have to wait outside until she called us, and only one boy at a time was going to be admitted. This puzzled the gang somewhat, but we agreed to her wishes.

The first boy she called into the lair was a lad called Bob who seemed to come out a lot faster than he went in. Next up was a guy called Gary, and he didn't last much longer than Bob. What on earth were these girls doing to these boys to make them scarper out of the den so quickly? Another lad called Chris loped in, but he stayed in for about thirty minutes. It was now beginning to get dark, and the remaining gang members were getting bored and curious. I noticed the flicker of a torch light from within the depths of the shelter, and realised that these girls had come prepared; obviously they were girl guides.

At last, Chris re-emerged into the evening air wearing a massive grin on his chops. I was beginning to think I was never going to be summoned into the sanctuary when to my relief, my name was called. As I entered, it was dark inside—but the stray beam from the torch allowed me to see Lynn and Lucy in the far corner of the den—minus their shirts. They were sporting only their bras, leaving an awful lot of skin on show. They noticed my gaping expression and told me that I had now entered the "Kissing Den". That was all well and good, but why had they removed their tops? Lynn then asked me to kneel down in front of her and put my arms behind my back. When I asked her why, she informed me that if I touched her tits she would kill me. Why did she think I wanted to touch her breasts? A million questions were whizzing around in my mind, but no answers were forthcoming.

"Shut your eyes, and purse your lips, Alf. I'm going to let you kiss me," Lynn said. I did exactly as she asked, and I began to get very excited. I could scent her perfume and commented on how nice it smelt. When I asked her what it was, she said, "Its soap, you thick twat. You should try it sometime!"

I was not going to be put off by her cold remarks and decided to limit my conversation to nothing. I started to feel warm all over, and I could sense her skin as it softly caressed my cheeks. Her lips parted as she connected with mine, darting her tongue into my mouth, then everything went tits up.

Because the night was drawing in, coupled with my new allergy, hay fever, just as our lips met in perfect synchronicity, I sneezed straight into her face. Not a normal little sneeze, but a fucking whopper that blew her teeth out. She screamed out loud in total fright at my nasal explosion, and all the other lads clambered in to see what was wrong. Her face was a picture. Thick snot was strung right over her cheeks like the mark of Zorro.

She went absolutely ballistic with me, smacking me in the mouth with her clenched fist. To make matters worse, everyone was laughing and this incensed her even more. She grabbed me by the ear and twisted it all the way round whilst kicking me on the shin. I had gone from delirium to depression in a nano-second, and I knew that worse was still to come. Wiping her face with my shirt, she spontaneously burst into song, surprising everyone there. Her song choice seemed a little ambiguous at first, but on hearing it for the second time, I knew instantly what I was in for. The song went as follows:

> Hicky picky marzipan, green snot pie,
> All mixed up in a dead dog's eye,
> Slap it on thin, slap it on thick,
> Swill it down with a cup of cold sick.

When I was growing up, certain geeky kids were made to go through a horrendous ritual of having to drink the collective mucus, or snot as we called it, of other bullying gang members for their sadistic pleasure. The thought of this still makes me retch to this day. Even though Lynn had the beauty of Mary Poppins and skin as soft as a baby's arse, she did possess a vile and vindictive temper. I had started to dote on this girl and was totally love struck. She was both seductive and alluring, but the hideous concept of swallowing her nasal slime was too much for me to bear. My passion ran deep—but so did my feelings of escaping this nightmare.

In a moment of sheer madness, I pulled down my trousers, squatted down on the floor, and proceeded to have a dump. It didn't take any coaxing or forcing—it came forth at pace, letting off a putrefying aroma in the course of its journey into the world. As luck would have it, everyone including Lynn made their respective getaways, leaving me there to ponder my fate. It was the longest crap in the history of man, but it saved my bacon that night.

I never saw Lynn again, as her family moved up north the following week. I did see Lucy, however, who was somewhat happy to see me. I explained my behaviour to her on that fateful night, informing her that every time I got excited, I needed to take a shit— and boy, was I excited that particular evening. With me, overexcitement and fear run hand in hand, and this creates a catalyst within me for the onset of diarrhoea. She seemed happy with my frank explanation and never mentioned the fateful sneeze, saying she thought it was because I was an "uphill gardener," slang for homosexual. Her assumptions were based on the fact that I'd not kissed Lynn properly.

Now supplied with the truth about my dilemma after I had managed to give Lucy reasons behind my bizarre actions, she kissed me on the cheek and told me she would see me around sometime. This small act of kindness ignited my inner passion, and I was seized with an urge to grab her attention.

As she started to walk away, I mustered up all my courage and beckoned her back by saying, "I think I'm falling in love with you."

She stopped in her tracks and turned to face me. I was glowing like a furnace, heart pounding like a steam train, beads of sweat began to forming on my brow … and there and then, my knackers dropped. Suddenly, my voice was deeper, I felt stronger and taller, and lo and behold, I got "a little fat lad on" in the trouser department.

Slowly she glided towards me, and carnal thoughts of *breaking my duck* (take a giant leap into the unknown) and popping her cherry at the same time in several short, rhythmic thrusts entered my brain, which had now become one with my bollocks. I'd never felt like this before and stood there power-less to her girlie charms. I was throbbing and aching all over and on the verge of creating some "funny wee" when she uttered the immortal words that will stay inside my heart forever.

"Alfie, you're just a boy in a man's world. Wait a year or two, and I promise to give you a good going over."

At this, she vanished into thin air, and I woke up.

Lucy featured in my next thousand "Sherman tanks"—and for that I am truly grateful– as is my optician. I had to wait a further agonising year to fulfil my urge of opening the sacred clam, but that's a tale for another day.

Now, going back to the dual themes of garden-ing and homosexuality, I would like to end this story by finishing off with a common phrase used by gay onion growers all over the world and say, with a tear in my "one-eyed trouser snake":

"That's shallot, darlings!"

Notes on Names and People

Throughout my first fourteen years, my late Grandad supplied me with a vast amount of background information and opinion, all of which I implicitly believed to be true. Therefore I have subsequently written down what I was told, never questioning his wisdom and rhetoric.

Childhood friends' names have been mixed with those from friends in later years and in places their personalities were spiced up a bit to create interesting characters.

Descriptions of people included in the story are part truth, part fiction, at times taking on traits and idiosyncrasies from other people I have had the good fortune to meet in my life. The actual events are all true, but not necessarily in the same order that they took place.

About the Author

Dene Lindley lives in a small village in South Yorkshire. He enjoys being outdoors, surrounded by nature, and all her beauty. It is here where he feels totally at ease with the world. Dene is a gregarious person who has been described by his children, as a cross between Billy Connolly and Spike Milligan. He has lived with depression for over twenty years, which he caught off one of his friends whilst playing out in the garden. His creativity occasionally tips him over the edge of reason, but his thirst for knowledge shows no bounds. He once read the dictionary backwards with his eyes shut. His characteristics and idiosyncrasies help make up a complex individual, who is always able to laugh at his misfortunes and constant bad luck. He would like this book to be an inspiration for hay-fever sufferers throughout Siberia.

Printed in the United Kingdom
by Lightning Source UK Ltd.
133898UK00001B/118-303/P